HEALING AMERICA

RICHARD BLOUNT IV

WESTBOW
PRESS°
A DIVISION OF THOMAS NELSON
& ZONDERVAN

WestBow Press books may be ordered through booksellers or by contacting:

WestBow Press
A Division of Thomas Nelson & Zondervan
1663 Liberty Drive
Bloomington, IN 47403
www.westbowpress.com
844-714-3454

ISBN: 978-1-6642-1418-7 (sc)
ISBN: 978-1-6642-1419-4 (hc)
ISBN: 978-1-6642-1417-0 (e)

Library of Congress Control Number: 2020923465

Print information available on the last page.

WestBow Press rev. date: 12/31/2020

Mission: A desire to develop optimism and hope in each citizen of America. To recover the peace for Americans through an understanding of our challenges in culture, politics, religion, media, and race. To present a new set of eyes to help us navigate and progress relationships to a healthier state of being.

Healing America covers the problems, causes, solutions, and benefits of being an American. We will investigate the history, culture, perceptions, responsibilities, and challenges that come with those topics. The book shares alternatives to vindication, like listening, humility, and empathy to yield healthy relationships as the ultimate goal. We must be intentional and purposeful with a vision of the healing process.

Lastly, the book delivers the benefits of being a part of America and the joy that comes with the opportunities we share in this country. Let us have friendship and fellowship together, love one another, and grow. Let us heal, America.

I dedicate this book to my supportive and loving wife, Gwendolyn Blount, who has brought so much joy to my life. I also dedicate this book to my three wonderful kids Bella, Cam, and Tori. I would like to dedicate this book to my wonderful parents, Richard and Rhonda Blount, who have given me such a great support and a great example of work ethic, and service to others.

PREFACE

In 2009, I took over a team of service reps at AT&T. I was given a profile update of one of the associates who would be on my new team. I was advised that this associate, James, was a challenge to manage. The profile given was a highly intelligent, fast learner—but a negative attitude.

Once I could get my entire new team into their new cubicles, in a designated area close together, I called in James to speak to him about putting him in a position of leadership on the team. I asked James if he would mind taking on the task of hyping up the sales team and keeping them focused on sales objectives throughout the month. I started out this meeting with James by honoring his positive attributes and explained that the purpose of this meeting was to recognize his strengths and put them to work within the team.

I gave James all the WIIFMs ("What's in it for me?") and he just stared at me and smiled. I was thinking the conversation was going better than I thought it would, and when I finally unraveled most of the conversation and the idea to James, I asked him how he felt about it.

James looked at me and started laughing. "I know what you are trying to do."

I looked at James, sort of confused, and thought, *There is no way you know what I am trying to do because only I know my strategy in this approach.* I had not shared this idea with anyone yet and acted on it quickly by just using some common manager coaching techniques I had read about.

I said, "James, what is it that you feel I'm trying to do?"

James responded, "You are trying to *grow me.*"

I thought, *Wow! How did he figure that out so quickly? James's profile did say he was highly intelligent.* I said, "James, what makes you think that?"

James said, "You are trying to *grow me*—and I do not want to grow." James had sort of completely crushed my plan to gain an ally to lead this team and diffuse any opposition on the team. James was right. I was hoping to *grow* him to be a positive impact on the team. I thought, *What type of person does not want to grow? Wow!*

James said, "I do not want to grow."

This is the *target* in this book. It is time to grow. Who doesn't want to grow? It is a meeting with America—to honor America's talent, diversity, and cultures, and to encourage America to grow. How many James's do we have today? From the start of this adventure, I hope we have individuals who want to grow. Let us open our hearts and minds to this time-share of thought throughout the pages of this book.

Let us begin. Has America lost its way? Is the character of the current day a representative of extraordinary art or a care-needed fixer-upper? What is the temperature of America today? Why is there so much opposition in America? The question is massive yet elementary, and surprisingly, everyone has some version of their own answer to it all. Every solution could be unique, and every answer is somehow wrapped around us, us, us, and they, they, they. Us and they are born opponents.

After careful observation of world news today, we Americans get a daily dose of opposition. The opposition has become a part of our diet. Life is how I see it, and if you do not agree, then you are wrong. Liberty and freedom are dear friends, but even they do not always get along. Freedom declares it set us free, and liberty states, "I want to be free." There is no liberty without freedom, and liberty must manage herself. Liberty and freedom cannot heal until they become "we." "We the people" was the most powerful statement ever recorded. Let's together take some time to review the "they" and the "us" and allow "we" to replace the separation we experience from "they" and "us". The we of America will be the hero that us and they tried to destroy. Team America, who wants to join while we begin to heal?

INTRODUCTION

An animated thought of Lady Liberty in a hospital bed crosses through my imagination. At the side of her bed, I see an elephant, and on the other side, I see a donkey. As I look more closely, I see a police officer. I then see a young Black man with his pants sagging down, showing his boxers, and I think, *Please pull those up, son.*

I then see an American soldier patting the back of a football player. I see a nurse holding a tray full of opioids, Xanax, and antidepressants, recommending that these things will help you cope, Lady Liberty. I see a

Bible on the floor at the foot of the bed, but no one seems to notice it or pick it up.

As Lady Liberty lays in her designated hospital bed, she ponders the events that have made her terminally ill. She also considers the moments of triumph in her life. As Americans began to stop respecting each other and showing empathy toward one another, she lost her strength and weakened.

Many say the stages of death take you back to the memories of childhood with family, friends, and loved ones. Some say your life flashes before your eyes. Lady Liberty is taken back to a place and time of accomplishment when she prevailed over British rule to become independent. She wowed the world for years with her Stars and Stripes, her military, her heroes, her athletes, her tech minds, and with her way with humanity around the world.

She has held a special place in the hearts of so many globally. Has she lost her care? Has pride had its way as a virus sickened her and negatively affected every function once thought of as inspired by God? One nation under God. In this vision, there are many in the room who are saddened by her sickness, and they are posturing in such a way to avoid seeming vulnerable.

The doctor finally enters the room and asks everyone in the room a serious question: "Do you want to heal?"

Many in the room look at Lady Liberty and wait for an answer. The elephant and donkey look at her. The football player looks at her. The police officer stands up and waits for her to answer.

The doctor says, "I am speaking to all of you in this room. Do you want to heal?"

Everyone hesitates. Behind the answer to this question could be something no one is ready for. To answer this question could require something of themselves. In this dream or moment of imagination, I thought of a Bible passage.

The Healing at the Pool on the Sabbath

> Some time later, Jesus went up to Jerusalem for one of
> the Jewish festivals. Now there is in Jerusalem near the
> Sheep Gate a pool, which in Aramaic is called Bethesda

and which is surrounded by five covered colonnades. Here a great number of disabled people used to lie—the blind, the lame, the paralyzed. One who was there had been an invalid for thirty-eight years. When Jesus saw him lying there and learned that he had been in this condition for a long time, he asked him, "Do you want to get well?"

"Sir," the invalid replied, "I have no one to help me into the pool when the water is stirred. While I am trying to get in, someone else goes down ahead of me."

Then Jesus said to him, "Get up! Pick up your mat and walk." At once the man was cured; he picked up his mat and walked. (John 5:1–9 NIV)

This took place on the Sabbath. The man at the pool was asked a yes-or-no question—just like the people in the room with Lady Liberty.

Finally, the donkey says, "We can't heal because they are not letting us."

The elephant says, "You people are all emotional and think everything has to go your way."

In the Bible passage, the man at the pool also hesitated to answer Jesus. He gave an excuse about why he had not yet been healed, and he blamed it on others. I'm sure others in the room felt similar to the elephant and the donkey. It is a simple yes-or-no question. Who would not want to be healed?

The doctor seemed frustrated that it took so long for an answer, and then the answer he got was not just a simple yes.

Lady liberty looked at each person in the room. "The answer to that question reveals where your heart is today. How long it takes you to answer will reveal how far you have to travel. Nothing will reveal if you are sincere in your answer unless you get up and do something. Insanity is doing something the same way and expecting a different outcome. You have done your business the same way for years, and it seems to have always expected a different result, but there is one game changer in every aspect of life. That is love and understanding. Do you want to heal? Yes or no. If your answer is no, then the message will not help at all. If the answer is yes, then let's proceed and see if we can grow. Doctor, help us all."

CONTENTS

SECTION I THE PROBLEM

Social Challenge Section 1

Film and post to social media a vacation you went on to see some historical sites in America. Share a demonstration of respect for that history with friends and family. Expand on what it means to be an American—and do not leave out the dark truths and bright sides. Remember that dark truths build character. We must grow through what we have gone through in America.

History is important; let's learn together. Point out what is real and how this history may have affected Americans in a positive way. Pressure must hit the coal before it yields a diamond. With more Americans sharing history, a sense of pride will start to educate and rebuke the powers that are against this great country. We must be sure this pride in America does not become idealized and is simply being shared to help us grow in gratitude for our home, which is the United States of America.

SECTION II THE CAUSE

Social Challenge Section 2

Identify your negative, which does not allow America to be great or you to be great. What are you ashamed of? This takes courage to share, and it also takes humility. Share on social media and ask for forgiveness, make it public, and then post what steps you will take to work on those areas of your life to become a better citizen, teammate, friend, family member, employee, church member, or neighbor. Being humble is one of the most potent characteristics one can have. We must show it.

SECTION III THE SOLUTION

Social Challenge Section 3

Make a video karaoke singing "Can You Feel It" by the Jackson 5. Invite friends, coworkers, teammates, or anyone else in your social arena. Make it hype, fun, and energetic, send a message with the music, and sing with some passion. We will set up a GoFundMe page so people— even celebrities—can contribute, and at the end of 2021, we will reward someone with the money from the GoFundMe donations; 50 percent will go to the winner, and the other 50 percent will go to the charity of the winner's choice. An organization could win or a single person. You can submit your performance from YouTube or TikTok.

SECTION IV THE BENEFIT

Social Challenge Section 4

Take someone who has different views from you out to lunch twice. Maybe you two are of different political parties, religions, or races. Identify a person you know for sure you may not have a lot in common with and invite him or her out to lunch. Then you must do it a second time. That person also has to invite someone out twice who he or she has identified. No matter who you invite out for lunch, you pick up the tab both times. Post a picture of the outing on social media and briefly explain why you chose that person and anything else you would like to share about the time spent with him or her. Try to learn and have a dialogue about current events and get to know each other. Allow peace and love to have a moment in the encounter.

SECTION I

THE PROBLEM

ONE

HISTORY AND CULTURE

The battle for America is between the *Donkey, the Elephant, and the Lamb.*
In Christ we become companions and not competitors. Can the *Lamb* win
our hearts? Man is the most unique species of the field in that he has the

ability of choice. I once heard a story of Christians often being defined by a breakfast sandwich. The chicken donated the *egg*, the cow donated some *milk* for the *cheese*. The pig donated his life for the *bacon*. Jesus Christ gave his life for a message of *love, sacrifice,* and *service*. We often as Christians have only given a portion of ourselves for the cause of Christianity and not yield our fullness to the cause. These three components of *love, sacrifice*, and *service* bring peace and reduce self-importance. The beauty we have before us today, is that there is still time decide which animal wins. Does the *Lamb* win? Then we get to decide what category of Christian we are. Are we just the Chicken donating an egg to the cause? Maybe we are the Cow and we give some milk for the cheese. Possibly the greatest food group of all times, a portion of bacon that was offered by the life of the pig. I pray that I did not disgust any Muslims. We have always been in position to heal and no election or elected official decides that. This is a decision that each American must decide on personally. It may require some love. Possibly will require some sacrifice, which means to give up something great, for something greater. Lastly, it will require some service from each of us towards our fellow American, no matter the background they come from, love thy neighbor.

In the first 3 chapters we will speak to the problems of our current challenges in America and I would like to kick this off by sharing a story that happened to a close friend of mine whom I will speak of again in my last chapter of this book. In 2016 a close friend of mine named Jammer received a promotion to a 3rd line status with his company. A moment that he had waited on for some time and an email was sent out to the organization to celebrate and recognize his promotion. This email came without notice and without a previous discussion of consent from Jammer. He thought how confusing, but he was grateful for the promotion. Many would come to his cubicle to congratulate him. He received instant messages from various platforms and text messages as well congratulating him. He was excited and happy, but still some confusion was setting in with Jammer. *"Why would a promotion be sent out for me to the corporate organization that had not yet been discussed with me in full detail of the merit of pay increase, requirements, and or even an acceptance."* Finally, Jammer got a chance to speak to his VP who was the boss of his boss. The VP told Jammer that he would send him an acceptance of the promotion in email for him to sign off on. He told his VP thank you and that he was very thankful. Jammer would later speak with his boss about the promotion and she shared with him that he should have been presented with the full detail of the promotion before it was sent to a VP. Jammer is African American. His boss is also African American and a female. Jammer's VP is Caucasion. Jammer felt as if this might have unfolded in this fashion due to his race. Later that day his boss came to him and apologized to him that he had to experience this in this fashion, and that it was not handled appropriately and more than likely it happened this way because he is African American. After lunch that day, Jammer finally received the email with the details of his promotion and was able to review the items that he should have received before his recognition email. You see if Jammer does not accept the promotion, then it would be an embarrassment for him in the office at this point. He was receiving some pressure from this thought. Jammer went to review his promotion offer with his boss who does not have view into the details, but she did approve of the decision to promote him. Jammer shows his boss that his offer is a very low with his promotion. He would also be given a few more accounts and his total responsible revenue would grow to seventy million annually with a monthly quota increase in to one percent of that total revenue each month. Jammer's boss told him that she feels this is offensive and degrading. She shares with him again that she apologizes for how he is being treated and that it is typical from this VP in how they treat African Americans. Jammer walked out of the office back to his desk and was trying to keep his temperature down. A day that seemed to start out so bright, with such a blessing in email, suddenly turned into the day of dread and Jammer's heart was crushed. Jammer pondered the blood, sweat, and tears he had given his position within his organization and felt he deserved the decency of a meeting prior to the promotional email coming out and also that he deserved much more on his promotion salary that represented his efforts and additional accounts he would now be responsible for. Jammer was getting angrier by the minute, with thoughts of walking away from the company he had now been with for 20 years. Maybe it's time to go now, he thought. Jammer went home for the day. Once at home he struggled to find peace and he shared with a few of his friends that were Caucasion about his experience and each of them without a doubt felt that this was direct discrimination towards Jammer, and they were equally apologetic towards Jammer's experience. Later that night one of his friend's wife called Jammer and advised him that he should seek legal action against this and that he deserves better.

Jammer is now fully stressed and could not sleep at all that night. He decided he was going to go into the office the next day and not accept the promotion or accept the promotion without an extended commitment to stay in this department for two years. You see this promotion came with a time commitment that he would not accept any other offers for the next two years. Jammer prayed and prayed for guidance on his response and attitude. Jammer was very spiritual and had been raised in the church. The next day came and Jammer did not want to go to work, but he gained some strength after his prayer and ventured on to work. Jammer entered his VP's office and had this look on his face of disgust.

His VP asked him *"what is wrong Jammer, you look really bothered."*

Jammer responded, *"I do not believe I can accept this promotion"*. "I believe this should have been discussed with me in advance of the email that went out to the organization."

The VP said *"Jammer, I apologize that I did not call you in before we sent the email out that morning. That was totally my fault. I had 24 hours to discuss with you and you had left for the day. We did speak of a promotion coming and I had been working on this for about 3 months for you. I felt you deserved it. You worked hard for me and this organization and I felt you were well deserving of it."*

Jammer, *"If I was deserving of it, then why was the amount of the raise so very low?"*

VP *"We cannot discuss the amounts of the raise. We never do that."*

Jammer, *"I will only accept the raise if I can be allowed to search for another position within the next year and be released to that position if I receive an offer."*

VP *"Jammer this promotion is an investment in you, and we would not want to let you be released that soon."*

Jammer *"A minor investment as it is, is nothing."* "I am worth more than that. That it is an insult and it is degrading. For all I have done for this organization and this company, never missing quota in the last four years and the thanks I get is a minimum raise and an email recognizing me for a

promotion as if it was a life changing achievement." "No thank you". Here is
your promotion and I am not interested, and Jammer walks out."

Later that day Jammer has another meeting with his Boss, and he asked her did he do the right thing. His boss advised him, that she was proud of him and that if no one stands up to their VP for his discrimination then others will face the same discrimination one day. His boss encouraged him, that he should file an HR report on the VP so that they do not try and fire him later. Jammer thought, *"Good Idea".* Jammer called the HR hotline and filed an HR complaint for discrimination. The HR agent asked Jammer had he first tried to discuss this situation with the President of the company, whom the VP reports to? Jammer said no, and that he would go and do that. Jammer setup a conference call with the President of the company to discuss the full measure of events around his promotion. Jammer started to feel somewhat better that maybe justice will be served from these efforts. He still felt bad that he was having to go through all of this, and his boss texted him a few times still apologizing that he has had this experience and was being discriminated against. Jammer had lived in such a way to avoid discrimination and approached his career with a polished extra-effort work ethic. It was disappointing that even that had not helped him to avoid discrimination.

On the third day Jammer had a conference call scheduled with the President of the company around 3pm. He scheduled it at the end of day, so that he can go home and dwell in misery if it did not go well. Around lunch time a peer of Jammer invited him to lunch and asked him why had not yet changed his signature line on his email to reflect his new title. Jammer explained to him the events that had transpired in the last two days and almost in tears has not accepted the promotion. This peer of Jammer was a spiritual man as well and said he wanted to pray with him about this situation. Jammer agreed and thought how odd this will be for two men to be praying at restaurant together in suits. After the prayer Jammer's peer told him that he had also met with the President of the company before, on a similar situation. This peer of Jammer was Hispanic. He told Jammer that the President of the company has full confidence in the VP and will not listen to any disparaging conversations about the VP. Jammer's heart dropped.

Jammer said, *"So this will probably not go well then?".*

His peer said, *I do not believe it will.*

Jammer's peer said *"this is not your - fight, get out the ring! Take the promotion and be grateful. God has the - fight now."*

Jammer's arm would need to be twisted for his frustration was at full strength, but being a spiritual man, he didn't just digest this as a peer speaking to him. Jammer perceived this to be God speaking to him, through his peer. *"Get out the ring"* he kept thinking. *"Get out the ring"*, *"It's not your fight".* The conference call with the President was near and Jammer had decided to change his approach. When he opened the conference call Jammer stated just the facts of the experience and nothing emotional or any opinions. *"Just the facts"* Dragnet style. Jammer's President said thank you for sharing your concerns and experience with me. His president apologized that the full view of what took place had not been shared with him. The President went on to tell Jammer that his VP had been fighting for this promotion for him for about three months and the reason it was taking so long, was that Jammer's sales results did not merit a promotion, but that his effort in retaining revenue did showcase a significant value to the company. Jammer was helping his module accounts that were mostly Energy, Oil, and Gas during a down-turn in production, retain revenue spend, and that it was hard to sale during these times. His President and VP both understood this and still agreed that beyond his sales results they should do something to recognize his efforts. The Company's HR department would not approve the promotion due to a company algorithm in place to stay consistent with all employees being recommended for a promotion. This standard keeps the company from making a personal decision on the promoting candidate and not being able to justify the pay increase in a legal battle. Jammer was shown that formula sheet and his regional ranking. He was then shown how this spreadsheet releases the raise amount. The President told Jammer that his VP fought for him each day for three months to just give Jammer something even though his results were not exactly in an elite status. Jammer was relieved to understand that he was not discriminated against. It no longer mattered if he would receive any pay increase, but that he was appreciated. Jammer had lost sight of just the value of being appreciated and recognized. The President of the company told Jammer that he would approve any position that Jammer was interested in within the next year and write him a recommendation for it. The President also explained to Jammer that he is a valued employee and that Jammer was being promoted and recognized during some challenging times in their industry, but he (Jammer) had done enough to deserve this promotion. Mostly everyone found it shocking that a promotion was released when the overall company had not performed well. Jammer maintained his base in his module and grew it slightly.

Later that evening Jammer called his peer and told him how the call went with the President. He thanked him for praying with him and his advice about *"Get Out the Ring"*. He said he will never forget that. It was not his fight. Jammer also opened his eyes to something else he learned. Not everyone you seek advice from has your best interest in mind and not everyone is spiritual minded. One input Jammer received from his boss was to get in the ring and fight. The advice he received from his peer was more spiritual and he was told get out the ring and let God fight. There was a strong perception here of discrimination and that Jammer was being treated unjustly. One adviser was driving the narrative of unjust and fight. Jammer's Boss was encouraging him to be vindicated, to justify himself. The desire to be vindicated in our current times is one of the direct causes of the unrest in America today. Another advisor was driving a narrative of prayer, peace, and to be grateful. Jammer would later go back and accept his promotion proudly, with humility, and apologize to his VP. He said he understood his confusion and frustration, but that they are not always allowed to showcase everything that took place, for fear that it may be shared with other employees and they might be offended. His VP said, I cried last night, and I am not a crying man. I was trying to understand how it went from promoting an employee to an HR filling on me for discrimination. I felt like I lost by trying to do something for someone I have a great deal of respect for. Jammer felt that he was mis-lead by his boss to fight a battle that she wanted fought. We live in some current times, that many are playing puppet master with society and driving perceptions and narratives that are not entirely truth. We have movement of *"the great manipulators"*. The media plays a role in this, and many of our nationally known Political Activists play a role in driving these responses to perceptions. These individuals, organizations and platforms have a similar approach as Jammer's Boss did. Some light fires and others just fan the flame. The public is normally the forest burning and they sit back and watch it burn as the first responders try and put out the fires.

Today's unrest and pains in America start with this simple process.

The Fire Starter

This is the person that has a strong desire for vindication and to be justified by their own opinions and set of beliefs. That may be democrat or republican. They find an angle on an issue and then they place that in dialogue to generate attention towards that propaganda. This may be news media and in most cases that is all it is.

The Flame Fanner

This is the person that normally is going to take that fire story and begin to spread it as evidence of some sort of conspiracy theory with partial facts, half-truths, due to their own interest in that subject matter. The Fan Flammer desires others to be interested as well. Yet it is all just political propaganda. They post it on their blogs, infomercials, social media accounts, and text message memes. These individuals cause more damage to the American peace that the actual fire starter. They are a fan of the political arenas and they are fire fanner. You know many of them and can identify them. They begin to add the editorials and emotions into what the fire starter begins.

The Forest

This is the public. Like a forest there is a diversity of trees and vegetation that burn at different rates. Those trees also thrive on different measurements of sunlight and water. The public is just as diverse and functions almost the same when it comes to what they are nurtured by and the acceleration in which they burn. The public or U.S. Citizen has no choice at times, but to stand and burn. Nowhere to run, because we live in America and we are going to get our news from somewhere. CNN, FOX, Social Media, etc.

The First Responders

The First Responders should be the mature, genuine, and faithful Christian. In many cases with the complexity of these dynamics, it requires that a first responder be someone who will "not" respond. First Responders are not limited to Christians, but I stated should be, because this would be required of Christians. Imagine that. The first responder to helping put out a fire is those that will not respond. They will get out the ring and not give in to the fight. Remember Jammer? They will use their citizenship to vote when appropriate and love their neighbor as themselves regardless of their political stances. The first responders help diffuse the fire, but not helping it continue to flame. We hope to build more First Responders. One can always listen to the Fire Starter and The Flame Fanner without responding. To not respond is a response and it's the most powerful response, because it counters the desire to keep burning. One can listen to learn and expand, but with self-control. One could grow in knowledge, but also in maturity to not continue the harm that is being done to the American Public. Which we have labeled the forest.

Let us get back to Jammer. Jammer really represents our current American Citizen. Being driven into the fight, by someone else's desire to be vindicated. He later understood that his boss did not like his VP and had it out for him for several other incidents that happened between them. Imagine that. We currently live in some-times that we must be careful of whom sympathizes with us and review if it is genuine or strategic? Different times. To gain allegiance with Jammer his Boss showed sympathy and empathy for his sad feelings towards the injustice he felt with the way the promotion was carried out. Jammer appreciated his Boss's understanding. This was not a response by Jammer's Boss to advance a sincere or genuine relationship with him, but to use him against someone he really dis-liked. Jammer realized that he was manipulated and used to fight that battle for his boss. He felt their relationship was violated. Jammer refused to fight again and even let that go. He was happy now, with just being appreciated. Years later Jammer would receive another promotion with a significant increase in pay and again and again in his career.

We are in some-times that everything is not what it seems, and perception can be different from what is truly reality. Many of Americans are being manipulated into a fight and into a political ring of battle with only a portion of the story understood. The narrative has be given to help render vindication to the desired party by means of drawing others into the fight or redemption. We have lost site to be grateful for the opportunities that we have. We are being drawn into the ideal of *"what we deserve"*. What we are intitled to. We only deserve fair opportunity. The media and politics embrace the strategy of driving narratives as a discipline, that cannot be compromised. If it is compromised, then this will reflect negatively on your commitment to that specific political movement. The political strategy is to embody fear in that fragile minds of society, and encourage the public to believe that fair opportunity, entitlement, and or God given rights are in jeopardy. The political strategy continues with another move and that is to create a posture of justification, vindication, and or no fight, no win. It is in our very nature to want to respond, with self-pride, to anything that threatens these areas. It is very natural. We must stay spiritual in these times. Take a step back to learn the history of all sides. You see it was the history of the situation that helped Jammer relax, lose fear, repent, extinguish the narrative, and free his own motives of vindication. Many Americans today are in one of these many positions of everyone portrayed in Jammer's story. It was "understanding" that gave him peace. Not everyone was against him. It was a friend that gave him the right advise. Let us place ourselves in a situation to understand the history of things, step back out the ring, and be grateful for the opportunities we have in America. Let us begin to heal through understanding. History if not understood can cause some problems and culture can yield to the perception of that history if not transparent or apparent.

I would like to pivot and begin our journey into Healing America. The Healing of America starts with being able to accept a culture and history we may not be able to agree with. It begins with understanding what started in good intent and later arrived at some darkness, was the only path to the opportunities we have today. Many in the bible faced some dark days. Joseph, Moses, Job, Noah, etc. Those dark days were meant to yield a prosperous fruit that would last a lifetime. No sacrifice by any persons will go un-noted by God himself in the book of life.

A significant portion of Healing America will be to start back at our own History and understand the Cultures that started from our History and then re-grow our pride in our own Country whether bad or good, it is us. The word *"We"* is powerful, and it is inclusive. Americans must think in the *"We"*. We accept family unconditionally and it is time to accept the American History unconditionally and move forward. We can design a Nation we can all be proud of. Not a perfect nation, but one we call home and that we are proud of no matter what. This doesn't mean we forget the past, but we release the pain and power it holds over us. Remember forgiveness is not about the person who caused the harm, but it is to heal the person that feels harmed.

Remember in the movie *"Back to the Future"* or in the movie *"Frequency"* when they would visit the past, they would alter the future. It can become a vicious cycle of correction. If we went back in History and just got rid of Christopher Columbus for all the bad things he had done, would we be at Baseball games today during the week at 2pm with large hot dog, favorite beverage, and peanuts? Would we have had the opportunity to watch our kids play in basketball games and hit the winning shot? Would we gather for Christmas and worship as we pleased on Sundays? How much would we alter by negating every person that was a part of America's dark history? Were they not just as much a value to our History as it has turned out?

History and *culture* are terms that have great value in each country and in each nation, but these terms also have vast differences in their meanings. Many use these words synonymously with each other and think they are the same. There are distinct differences between the two terms. History records growth, nongrowth, a timeline of events, significant changes in laws, morals, and culture in a country or land.

Culture reveals the interests shown by the people of that country or land. History deals specifically with the past. Culture showcases the past and what has survived and is still relevant today. History and culture are pillars in perception, how we view things, and how we make decisions.

The only thing that conquers history and culture in the decision-making realm is wisdom through applied knowledge, and this comes with a high level of emotional maturity or maturation in life skills.

On a vacation to Boston on the Fourth of July in 2017, my family and I were able to digest some rich history of America. We went on a duck tour in Boston and visited Salem, Massachusetts. I was unfamiliar with how much rich history is in Boston and being able to see the pioneers' efforts and challenges inspired and moved us. I began to appreciate all the hard work of Americans and what has been accomplished in this country to get it to the place it is today.

In Boston I was able to visit Christopher Columbus Park and see a statue of him. I thought to myself, but Christopher Columbus never visited Boston Massachusetts or even this portion of America. Why did he gain credit for such a great accomplishment? What courage a man must have to set out on 4 separate voyages across the Atlantic during those times with limited technology. Christopher Columbus landed in the Bahamas, South America, Central America, and Caribbean. Christopher Columbus arrived in the Bahamas around October 12, 1492. Christopher Columbus only lived into his fifties. How much damage could one do in such a short life? Over a hundred years later the Mayflower bringing Pilgrims and Puritans arrived in Massachusetts on November 21, 1620. They were at sea for 10 weeks with 102 individuals who sought to reform the Church of England. In 1620 this group set for the Promised Land in America and established Plymouth Colony. Christopher Columbus did not truly discover America. The Indigenous people had been living here in America for centuries. Leif Eriksson and the Vikings arrived five centuries sooner than Columbus. The Vikings did not seize the opportunity to dominate the land and will their influence onto its culture during that time. Later it would be the English Families upon the Mayflower that would dwell and celebrate "Thanksgiving" with their newfound neighbors. Even their arrival was very close to what would be Thanksgiving.

While I was in Boston on a speedboat ride called Codzilla, I thought about a huge ship, the Mayflower, landing in the harbor of the new land. You are off the high seas, but now you must survive and explore. I'm sure this was the normalcy of this time, but also consider how cold it gets in Boston and how quickly one must adjust to survive.

Here is Lady Liberty's start. She is courageous. She must "get 'er done." Lady Liberty did not colonize for some hundred years. The English culture has now arrived in North America. To later establish what would be America. The simplicity of Christopher Columbus's influence on America was just the exploration of the Atlantic and identifying there was more land across it. So why should we recognize him? Well it is often thought if it were not for his continuous voyages, that maybe the English would not have had the courage to do so as well. Christopher Columbus's history beyond these voyages is very dark. He enslaved the Indigenous people and treated them with great violence. This could have been out of fear or defense of his own safety or just out of pure spite. Much blood was shed during his arrivals at new land.

When we consider those who knew the man and documented the events, is it not fair to say that Christopher Columbus has earned some merit or esteem from his courage? At the time, the indigenous peoples were not documenting history in the form that resembles what has been handed down today, and there was no real American culture as we know of today. Christopher Columbus established the opportunity for American culture to unfold. One portion of history and a separate portion to come is culture. There is dark history with the killing of indigenous peoples and slavery that has scared many Americans, but what culture does not have a dark side? Let's even rephrase that to say *who* does not have a dark side that helped mold their character and strength today? We all do. It is a part of life that no one can escape unless we just grow in a box where no harm is done, but even then, what would our character be like and what strength would we have? History includes kings, leaders, presidents, and prime ministers—and the people those people governed. Culture has influence on art, music, drama, and dance. History covers the first recorded events up to current events. Culture is the pollination of all the experiences and the by-product of the inspired events.

One example of a historical event is the invasion of the Philippine shores by the Spaniards. Culture refers to the religion, art, dance, and other influences the Spanish invasion had on the country. History is made up of rulers, presidents, kings, and physical monuments and essential events, and culture is comprised of connoisseurs of all forms of art. History is about the creation of a nation or state; culture, on the other hand, is one of the results of history. History is a written record of the country or nation in chronological order, including public events or human affairs. Culture fosters the more creative and intellectual aspect of the nation's people.

One might ask, Why so much about Christopher Columbus? Why is this a part of the problem? In college, a Muslim (Nation of Islam) student advised me that history is really "his-story." I want to point out that there is a significant difference in belief structures between an orthodox Muslim and one who is studying under the leadership of the Nation of Islam. He was saying that history is not always factual because it is made up by those who recorded it.

As Napoleon once said, "What is history but a fable agreed upon?" History is typically written by the winners. When cultures are at war, the loser is belittled, and the winner often gets to write the history books. The history books will glorify the cause of the winner and disparage the character of the defeated culture.

Consider the Battle of the Alamo in Texas history. The Alamo was a Mexican mission owned by Mexico. Missions are places of worship, support, and charity for the regions they reside in. The Alamo was taken by Texans/Americans.

Santa Ana, the leader in Mexico, came to take it back, and with more than a thousand soldiers, he defeated the hundred or so brave Americans in a battle. Santa Ana allowed women and slaves to live. Most history books depict Santa Ana as a bad man who bullied and brutally slaughtered the Texans, but the truth is that the Alamo had been seized and stolen by the Americans. The land that is now Texas was stolen by the Americans. Most of those who died at the Alamo are considered heroes, but were they really heroes? Were they not doing something that is regarded as evil?

In the Battle of San Jacinto, where Texas won and Santa Ana was defeated, the battle cry was "Remember the Alamo." The soldiers in Texas used the annihilation of their friends at the Alamo to fuel their efforts at San Jacinto. Why should we remember the Alamo if we were wrong in what was done at the Alamo?

Previously, Stephen F. Austin had made Santa Ana an offer for Texas. Santa Ana refused to sell Texas, and he placed Stephen F. Austin in jail. Stephen F. Austin was later released, and when he headed back to Texas, the Texans understood that the only way to get the land that would be called Texas was to take it.

With that said, let's consider Christopher Columbus. The Muslim (Nation of Islam) student followed this up with a thought-provoking question: "How did Christopher Columbus discover America when Indians or Native Americans were already here?" Well, the point we are evaluating here is that even the history of America was written to glorify the victor and not those who were defeated.

During that time in college, I was only eighteen, and I was not really the best debater or history expert. I thought, *That makes a lot of sense.* After years of careful examination of these questions, I started to realize that North American history and American history are two different histories. North American history includes the indigenous peoples, maybe the big bang (I don't believe in this theory), and the Ice Age. American history must start with culture because it is not a continent but a country. American culture has a birthplace. With the killing of the Native Americans and slavery, America may have several birth defects.

In America, we have recently removed the recognition of Columbus Day and have replaced it with Indigenous People's Day in some states. Notice I said "in America" and not "in North America." North America could include Canada, but America alone cannot. America includes Hawaii, but North America does not.

Culture often will supersede material rights. For example, each state has its own culture. I am a Texan, and boy, are we proud. We can be arrogant. We call ourselves the Lone Star State, and we declare that everything is more prominent in Texas.

Louisiana, our neighboring state, is a "game state" with cuisine to die for. One hundred miles in one direction will get you chicken fried steak and mashed potatoes, and one hundred miles in the other direction will get you gumbo, crawfish, and fried alligator. Louisiana has its land history, which is different from most of the other states in the Union, and it has a cultural history.

Indigenous people represent so much about the United States, but the indigenous peoples cannot gain credit for organizing the United States and giving birth to Lady Liberty and the cultures that we have today. Christopher Columbus is a part of the awakening to that history. The indigenous peoples are as well. While the Europeans/British were organizing about the Thirteen Colonies on the Atlantic Coast back to the Appalachian Mountains, in Louisiana, the French were settling along the Mississippi, and the Spanish were settling in Florida. Many French and Indian wars took place in those areas.

The British also evoked additional taxes on these colonies as they organized, and this sparked the resistance. We can review the Stamp Act and the Boston Tea Party regarding the tax resistance, but while I was in

Boston, my family and I got a chance to see the Boston Tea Party Museum. We also visited Paul Revere's House Museum.

We visited the very balcony where the Declaration of Independence was signed, and I tried to imagine what that day must have been like for the people. What blood, sweat, and tears went into getting to that moment. My contemporary version of this moment was more like an NBA Championship. I pictured men in White wigs popping bottles of champagne in a locker room with stockings on.

Can we agree that there is no America without this moment? It is part of our own history as Americans of any race. Many cannot so much relate to the indigenous people's history, but we understand that it is essential, should be respected, and has suffered some unfortunate events throughout American history. Understanding brings peace. It does not mean we agree, but we can have enough knowledge of the big picture. Let us grow through what we know.

A visit to Boston is incredibly helpful for understanding why this city has always been so proud of its franchises and its strong culture. I believe every American should be required to visit Boston for a week to absorb how we got to be America. There are some ugly stories behind it and some unjust moral issues in the history, but none of our daily pleasures and pastimes happen without Columbus or Boston.

We must embrace history and culture and try to respect what good came from it. Remember, each region of the United States has its own culture. The South has a culture, and the West has a culture. Texas has a culture, and Florida has a culture. The Midwest has a culture, and the Northwest has a culture. These cultures drive perceptions, thoughts, decisions, responses, and an assortment of behaviors.

To try to gain peace in America, we must discern cultural influences, areas, regions, and values so that we can collectively try to gain an understanding of effective communication with each other. A governor must understand the culture of their state to be a successful communicator. The president must understand all those cultures to be successful/effective in speech. Each president should be required to go through a diversity and inclusion study in the first week in the office or as a prerequisite for running for president. The greatest idea will have the most significant harm if the tone is insensitive to the cultures that are listening.

Boston is not the only culture, and it is not the dominant culture, but I believe it has to be considered in the overarching culture of America and how it originated. Each region has its own rich culture that materializes its people's thoughts and concerns. A boss once said, "I am always in agreement with what you said, but I am rarely in agreement with how you said it." My boss added, "You have the hammer, but you don't have to show it—and every job doesn't require a hammer." This simple statement helped me so much in my delivery and approach with my team and those who reported to me.

Much of the harm today in the United States is due to a lack of understanding of cultures and regions and a lack of knowledge of the perceptions of those cultures on the national news. We often show the hammer, and it's not always needed to effectively deliver a point—and we are insensitive to the cultures that are listening. Political leaders should try to gain an abundance of intelligence around culture and materialize an approach to be gentle toward everyone's culture and perceptions. This can often be accomplished by first honoring the culture of the audience. Through honor, we gain trust and respect because we have shown confidence and respect. We can soften the hearts and ears for receiving a message of encouragement, direction, development, and even correction. I was more a great communicator than I was an effective communicator. Once I understood personality traits, culture, diversity, and inclusion, I became more effective in leading, communicating, and encouraging.

What does God have to say? Let us examine Joseph in the Bible for a moment. Joseph was the son of Jacob, whose name was later changed to Israel by God. Jacob/Israel had twelve sons, and Joseph was his favorite. Joseph's brothers got very upset about this. They conspired against the boy and sold him to slave traders, and they told their father that he had been mauled by an animal. Joseph had been given dreams of God's plan for his life, and with confidence and strength, he endured in the amazing story in Genesis.

The slave traders took him into Egypt and sold him to Potiphar, one of Pharaoh's officers. Joseph served his master well and gained great favor, but the master's wife tried to seduce Joseph, a young man of impeccable integrity. After he rejected her, she went to her husband with false accusations. It resulted in Joseph's imprisonment. Once again, God proved his presence and protection for Joseph. The prison keeper befriended him and learned of Joseph's divine ability to interpret dreams.

Because of earning this reputation, Joseph was called upon to interpret a dream that deeply troubled Pharaoh. None of Pharaoh's wise counsels had been able to decipher the dream, but Joseph accurately relayed the symbols in the dream to a future time of abundance that would be followed by a time of great famine. Pharaoh rewarded Joseph with overseeing the lands of Egypt. In those prosperous times, he stored up the abundant harvest for the tragic times ahead.

During the years of famine, Joseph's brothers came in search of grains and food to keep their people from starvation. Not recognizing their young Hebrew brother as a mature and prominent Egyptian, he ordered them to return with their younger brother. When the brothers returned with Benjamin, Joseph revealed his identity. The brothers suffered from great remorse, and Joseph forgave them. He did not seek vindication for the things they had done to him. This is one of Joseph's most powerful statements:

> You intended to harm me, but God intended it for good to accomplish what is now being done, the saving of many lives. (Genesis 50:20 NIV)

It was a joyous reunion between a grieved father and lost son. Joseph's years of steadfast reliance on God brought about the reunion and his high position, and he was able to save a nation from starvation.

As we consider Christopher Columbus and the statues, and the holiday in his name, let us be reminded of Joseph and his statement to his own brothers. What the Pilgrims did to the Indians or indigenous people, they may have meant for evil, but as of today, God meant for good. When we think of slavery in America, did any good come from it? When we consider the American Dream Team walking up on the podium with the American flag draped over their backs in one of the proudest moments in American sports history and in African American history, would it even have been possible if there was no slavery? When we consider the forty-fourth president of the United States was an African American man, would it have been possible without slavery? We have not forgotten how awful slavery was, but what was meant for evil, but God may have meant for good. Look at the good in America and be reminded of the evils that had to transpire for us to get there. The next time you are enjoying a peaceful moment with your family, consider the sins of America and what good came from those errors today.

Adversity spawns' character and character is not achieved without adversity. For so it was with Joseph from the beginning in Genesis to be able to provide for his family through the famine. What would have happened if Joseph's brothers did not sell him into slavery?

The giant picture in this story is that Judah, one of the twelve brothers, was from the lineage of Jesus Christ. Joseph protected and provided for Judah, and Jesus the Christ would later come from that side of the family under Jacob (Israel). Joseph being sold into slavery is enormous when we consider this. If we needed to understand why, here is the heavy reason. The Bible—God's Word—knew what we would face from day to day, which would cause much confusion. God's Word provides wisdom to settle us down, bring calm, and bring peace.

Culture has great power, wherever it is home. In America, we have American culture, we have regional culture, we have state culture, and we have local culture. Texans have a strong state culture, and southerners have a strong regional culture. Boston's culture believes there is no you or the United States without Boston's culture.

History and culture are essential for getting to the root of the problem. Discernment of history is important as well. Perception becomes a reality in most of our worlds, and culture drives perception in many cases. It's how we *see* it and not always how we *are* that guides how we see things.

I'm an African American male, and there is no way I can relate to the culture of Boston, but when I opened my heart, I thought that Boston's history is my own American culture. For the African American male, the Mexican American male, the Indian American male, and the French American male, Boston's history becomes all our history. What Columbus meant for good, but frankly was evil, God turned it into good as history progressed. America is good.

TWO

WITH GREAT POWER COMES GREAT RESPONSIBILITY

Jammer realized that if he would have gone to his President of the company and made disparaging remarks about his VP and his perception of what he had done to him, that this could have been frowned upon and created a blemish on his own character. You recall his Peer said that the President of the company had a great deal of respect for the VP and that he (President) understood the efforts he (VP) had made to help Jammer gain the promotion. Jammer believed that his original intent for the meeting could have been career suicide and possibly harmed him from any future promotions. Not because he should not have stood up for himself, but because he had it wrong. God in many situations if one leads a prayerful life, will intervene to save us from ourselves. Jammer realized he had been recovered in a moment's notice, to humble himself prior to meeting with his President.

Six months later after these events, Jammer received a significant raise based on his new promotion title and he was well pleased with the amount. Once he added it all up, the amount was more than he originally expected from the promotion. *Do good things come to those who wait? Do good things come to those that work hard and stay humble?* The answer could be yes to both. Jammer has never forgotten the statement his spiritual friend had given him on that day before the call with his President. *"Get Out the Ring", "This is not your Fight".*

In America today, many should try and digest these same words. We are in a political fight of our lives it would seem, but why? Fear driving from both sides has the American Citizen believing their rights are at risk or in jeopardy. One of the most difficult growth sessions we are in as a nation right now is understanding the media's narratives towards each culture, from all political sides. The media has great power and they are drawing much of this up to sound and look a certain way depending on the strategy for a specific group. African Americans may feel like *"we have been hurt and oppressed so often we begin to have moments of relief that someone feels our pain".* The media is capturing a group in some vulnerable times and using that to drive emotions towards the perceptions that match the strategies of the political narratives. These perceptions have become reality for many.

We must begin to take a few steps back, analyze without emotions or historical feelings, and treat all the painful incidents on an individual case basis. If we come to the same place with the same conclusions no worries, but I doubt the verdict would be the same. I believe if we can discern each incident, then rise above the emotions, and eventually the media will lose its strong hold on each culture it has a strategy for.

Many Christians have given into the *political ideologies* and joined in these fights with a posture that is not representative of a Christian walk. They the Christian has joined in the fight as a Flame Fanner. Remember *"Love thy neighbor"? What if thy neighbor is a Democrat or a supporter of Black Lives Matter? What if my neighbor has a Trump flag in front of his home? Do we still love them?* Christ sees the soul and places a great deal of value on that soul. *What color is a soul?* Blood is all the same color. Even Christ's blood that saves. *Have you ever thought about that? Does a soul have a color? Then why are we concerned with color so much in America?* We are. *Is a professional athlete considered our neighbor?* They are if we do not know them. Neighbor is stranger. Culture and tradition can begin to gain greater value than the message of the cross. Politics place greater value on things of the world and less on kindness and consideration of the fellow man (neighbor). With that said let's begin to learn our 2nd point in our problem and that is with great power, comes great responsibility.

The Christian has great power and has a great responsibility to be the light of the world. A Christian's Power comes from God. They have the ability to tap into a higher power to bless others. Our leaders and people of authority have great power and a great responsibility as well. Great power in America is so often given certain immunities. In Romans 6:1 in the NIV version of the bible the Apostle Paul states *"What shall we say, then? Shall we go on sinning so that grace may increase?"* Power positions of Authority in America have some measure of immunity and much of this can be understood, but it should not allow for abuse of that power to increase the measure of immunity. Christians have grown silent on these examples over the years, if it's in agreement with their political ideologies, but Christians have grown louder in their political postures on social media, in public, and with their social network.

The 2020 Christian has made it more known of their political stance and less of their spiritual stance. Many Americans approach the day to attempt to drive out darkness with darkness. I'm sure it can be well documented that Christians do as well. Neither have understood that *"only"* love will conquer hate or at least have accepted this absolute. They often judge themselves by their intent, while judging others by their actions. Those guys whom you do not agree with are judging themselves by their intent as well and have not had hindsight to see their actions that you detest. The reason Martin Luther King gave this statement of hope and direction was to give something greater than theory or opinion on how a country and its people can heal. Martin drew this conclusion from Jesus the Christ (savior). Love thy neighbor as thy self.

We live in some dark times and each person each day is given the option and or opportunity to drive out darkness with light and hate with love. Instead many still have allowed a vindication and a desire to be justified in their opinions to yield its emotional head out front of their post and assertions, still attempting to *"drive out darkness with more darkness"*. The definition of insanity. Insane. Only, means singular. Only, light drives out darkness. Only, again means singular again. Love drives out hate. Are your *"social media posts"* Light and Love, or just opinion, political narrative, and judgement. One could self-reflect and self-check. *Ask yourself, "do I contribute to the darkness or the light"? Do I send love or judge hate? Ask yourself what side of the fight have I been on? "Darkness or Light"*. In Genesis 1:2-4 (NIV) 2 Now the earth was formless and empty, darkness was over the surface of the deep, and the Spirit of God was hovering over the waters. 3 And God said, *"Let there be light,"* and there was light. 4 God saw that the light was good, and he separated the light from the darkness.

Does America have a history that is arguably dark at times and arguably bright at times—but a culture of greatness the majority of the time? Can we agree? Spider-Man's uncle, Ben Parker, said, "With great power comes great responsibility." He was coaching Peter Parker to get involved and do what was right and use his talents to defend those who could not defend themselves.

If he had not gotten involved, then great tragedies could have occurred. Peter was given something great with his Spidey senses: power and ability. Peter was initially reluctant to use this power for good and serve. With this reservation, innocent people were harmed and left vulnerable to the outside world. Spider-Man's power would charge him with great responsibility.

Our president has such great power, and along with this power comes great responsibility. I pray for him from time to time that he will use this power wisely to help us grow as a nation. The process of growing is rarely without adversity, and at times, I realize that I have gotten what I have asked for in that prayer. Adversity is here. We cannot expect diamonds without the compression of coal, and in America, we cannot expect anything fruitful or rewarding without some pressure and pain. They go hand in hand. To expect some good is to expect some bad.

If we research further about "with great power comes great responsibility," we find the same quote utilized during the French Revolution. The following passage from May 8, 1793, was discovered within a suppository of the decrees made by the French National Convention:

> *Les Représentans du peuple se rendront à leur destination, investis de la plus haute confiance et de pouvoirs illimités. Ils vont déployer un grand caractère. Ils doivent envisager qu'une grande responsabilité est la suite inséparable d'un grand pouvoir. Ce sera à leur énergie, à leur courage, et surtout à leur prudence, qu'ils devront leur succès et leur gloire.*

> The people's representatives will reach their destination, invested with the highest confidence and unlimited power. They will show great character. They must consider that great responsibility follows inseparably from great power. To their energy, to their courage, and above all to their prudence, they shall owe their success and their glory.

Lord Melbourne, Winston Churchill, Teddy Roosevelt, and Franklin D. Roosevelt made similar statements. America has been blessed with great power in our culture, in our efforts (history), in our diversity, in our people, in our economy, in our opportunities, in liberty, and in freedom. Due to our many powers, we have many responsibilities.

In 1817, a debate was held in the United Kingdom's House of Commons concerning the suspension of habeas corpus. William Lamb spoke in favor of suspension. During the following decades, Lamb became a powerful political figure, and he ultimately emerged as prime minister. Lamb is now better known as Lord Melbourne. The transcript of Lamb's words in 1817 used quotation marks to enclose the maxim, indicating that the expression was already in circulation. Please note that the modern reader will find the style of the transcript atypical because it was presented from a third-person perspective. The referent "he" was used to identify the speaker, Mr. Lamb:

> It was common to speak of the power of the press, and he admitted that its power was great. He should, however, beg leave to remind the conductors of the press of their duty to apply to themselves a maxim which they never neglected to urge on the consideration of government: "that the possession of great power necessarily implies great responsibility." They stood in a high situation, and ought to consider justice and truth the great objects of their labors, and not yield themselves up to their interests or their passions.

There is freedom of the press, and the press has great power. Even the press has a responsibility to understand how their power influences the people who are vulnerable to the messages the press delivers. Some have no stable, secure thoughts about the news's content.

"Fake news" is a real thing that can affect actions that are not becoming of a progressive nation that is trying to heal. Can the press be the greatest threat to this nation? *After Truth* examines the threatening trajectory of disinformation (fake news) from Jade Helm to Pizza-gate to Russian interference in the 2016 election and many other headlines from the last decade. This documentary showcases an investigation into how ordinary people are radicalized, misguided, and manipulated by fake news.

One example of the damages and dangers caused by misinformation was a pizzeria that was caught in the crossfire of fake news. James Alefantis, the owner of a pizzeria, learned about a conspiracy theory surrounding his business from a reporter. In the days before the 2016 election, Will Sommer, then of the *Washington City Paper*, had been following a thread on Reddit in which shared emails from John Podesta, Hillary Clinton's campaign adviser, were used to justify an elaborate, yet entirely false story of a secret Hillary Clinton child abuse society happening in the back of Comet Ping Pong. James Alefantis had never heard of the false online hysteria, and this ludicrous theory, known as Pizza-gate, was launched.

This faux story caught traction and was propagated by Alex Jones, an infamous conspiracy theorist. Alex Jones begin to disseminate the story on Facebook and Twitter. Harassment of Comet Pizza and its staff ignited, and Yelp reviews began to reference child dungeons. Pictures of James's godchildren were posted on Instagram and were repurposed to attack him as a pedophile with specific, hateful references to his identity as a troubled man.

This nightmare spiraled out of control and prank callers began to issue death threats. On December 4, 2016, Edgar Welch, a twenty-eight-year-old man from North Carolina, convinced from online forums that he had to find the children himself, entered the pizzeria with an AR-15. Fortunately, no one was hurt, and the gunman was arrested, but the episode underscored the terrifying power of conspiracy theories and fake news articles that are cultivated in forums such as Reddit and 4chan and propagated by Facebook and Twitter. There are severe consequences. The bodycam footage from the DC Metro Police can be found online.

Brian Stelter, host of CNN's "Reliable Sources" and an executive producer of *After Truth*, talked to the *Guardian:*

> It shows how average Americans can be radicalized by content posted to the media, social media, and other platforms that freely allow fake news. The fake news content is powerful, and the media platforms have great power. People could have lost their lives in this particular experience and many have been tormented with the severity of the uproar behind the false news. It is important to understand the power behind the content on the internet was the driving force that motivated a man to get in his car with a gun (AR-15) and confront innocent citizens at a local family friendly frequented pizzeria. This is huge when you really wrap your thoughts around the power of the media platforms.

After Truth tracks the influence of disinformation and then conducts the CSI work to track down the origins of the content. *After Truth* analyzes the intent of the content and shows people deliberately disseminating "falsehoods" as opposed to "misinformation."

In 2015, Russian weaponization of social media platforms redirected public views during the 2016 election. We are living in times of some of the greatest falsehoods known to the public—or unknown to the public—in the history of modern journalism and media coverage. This consistent misinformation continues to manipulate people's imaginations. Even after they've been thoroughly debunked, investigated, and clarified, it has minimum impact on a change of perspective.

Andrew Rossi, a director from the *Guardian,* explained how the term "fake news" dates back to 2014 when Craig Silverman's BuzzFeed polarized it. Andrew used the phrase "fake news" to describe false stories about the Ebola crisis. *After Truth* begins in 2015 with online conspiracy theories wrapped around a military drill in Bastrop County, Texas. Known as Jade Helm, the theories, harnessed by YouTube personalities, spilled into Bastrop County's local life. Suspect footage began to depict an army spokesperson who was shouted down by people who dismissed his reassurances as propaganda. Instead, they believed an internet personality driven theory that there were underground tunnels connected to the Bastrop County's Walmart back to the military base.

The hysteria caught Texas governor Greg Abbott's attention, and from the start, he seemed to treat it seriously. Russia took notice. Russia saw the effectiveness of this driver to control behavior, fears, and beliefs and started replicating this pattern of news on many American social media platforms, heading into America's election year. Disinformation certainly ramped up in unison with Donald Trump's rise to the Republican nomination and, eventually, the presidency.

The president understood early about the effectiveness of this sort of battlefield of play. The weaponization of the term *fake news* against any opposing news outlets was a significant pivotal moment in 2017 that yielded a way to minimize the power of the media even when it could be true delivery of factual content. The president took the term and exploited it for his own political gain and/or used it for personal defense of unwarranted attacks. Today, fake news is America's greatest strategy for elections, votes, and movements. What is true? Only the astutely emotionally intelligent will know. For Comet Pizza, there was a happy ending. The loyal customers rallied around the business, keeping it open after they heard the truth wrapped around the false narratives.

The same happy ending cannot be said for the family of Seth Rich. The twenty-seven-year-old Democratic National Committee (DNC) staff member was killed in an unsolved botched robbery in the summer of 2016. Rich's death became fodder for online conspiracy theorists, and they baselessly linked the staff associate to some DNC emails that actually came by way of Russia that claimed murder by the Clintons. The Fox News host Sean Hannity ran a prime-time story boosting the Seth Rich conspiracy, which Fox News later retracted.

Aaron Rich, the brother of Seth Rich, has confessed to having to fend himself against internet social media trolls, and this battle has left him unable to grieve his brother's senseless death. *After Truth* explores how much of disinformation's power lies in human emotion. Fake stories are often successful when they capture their audience's heart in some way. There was a *Fire Starter* involved, there were also *Flame Fanners,* and then there was the *Public.* If there were more *First Responders*, this possibly would not have happened.

Another incident and investigation was launched with Jones and Jack Burkman, Washington lobbyists who hosted a press conference in 2018 with Jacob Wohl. The strategy was believed to be a smear campaign against Robert Mueller with an assault allegation that ended up falling short of its intended goal. The person in question or "victim" elected not to show up during a press conference.

During the press conference, tweets were sent that antifa had a chartered bus outside the press conference and was ready to attack the conservatives. It was discovered to not be true. A fake website was established with fake employees to showcase the validity of how the story was delivered from a reputable source. The employees' pictures were just models, and one was even a conspirator. Extreme lengths were taken to try and deliver a narrative that had no truth or facts behind it.

Who is the real enemy here though? Is it the public? Is it the media? Social media? Is it the individuals using the effective measures of these platforms to drive the behavior, thoughts, and fears of the public? Jack Burkman would later call disinformation a "tool of war." He said, "Like chemical weapons, if someone else can use it, I may as well use it too." There was a *Fire Starter* involved, there were also *Flame Fanners,* and then there was the *Public.* If there were more *First Responders*, this possibly would not have happened. Censorship of social media has been created due to the loss of life and dangers produced by false statements. Now due to social media platforms having great power as well, they now have a great responsibility to monitor those being ignited by the fire starters and flame fanners to be sure that the safety and healthy mental stability of the public stays in a safe place. Man will exploit anything he gets his hand on for any length of time. Now social media platforms or a portal of the most destructive thoughts and statements to break down our democracy and healthy minds sets of vulnerable Americans that cannot discern between fact and fiction. Adolf Hitler was one of the greatest motivational speakers of all times. Imagine Adolf with social media access during his time. Would he be censored? I believe America can say we did censor Adolf and went to war, to be sure his views did not advance. Censorship can be demonized as a method to restrict freedoms and liberties granted to us in America, but there are unique cases where it is the responsibility of those in power to govern or review its harm to open public. This is a space where capitalism and free speech will not agree with censorship and or bigger government with censorship. Balance is important and monitoring harm would be endorsed by Christian standards. Christians do not have freedom of speech but are required to speak only to build up by biblical standards. The Christian should be ok with censorship. As Christians we are censored by God himself through his word. Ephesians 4:29 NIV [29]Do not let any unwholesome talk come out of your mouths, but only what is helpful for building others up according to their needs, that it may benefit those who listen. Again, God has censored us from freedom of speech. We are respecters of the constitution and it's liberties, but they do not give us freedom compromise God's word. 1 Peter 4:11 NIV: If anyone speaks, they should do so as one who speaks the very words of God. If anyone serves, they should do so with the strength God provides, so that in all things God may be praised through Jesus Christ. To him be the glory and the power for ever and ever. Amen. Christians should not be open to censorship when it silences them, to share God's word. Evangelist. So often we are less passionate on God's word and much more passionate on political stances. It should be just the opposite and God's word is love thy neighbor.

There is no one solution for deescalating fake news, and there is no right answer. It would take an astutely emotionally intelligent person with a healthy measure of understanding of media literacy 101. Covid-19 has us directly in the midst of a once-in-a-generation pandemic in which correct, reliable information and public trust are now literally a matter of life and death. An understanding of the tools of disinformation, political narratives, and social media news platforms may be more important than ever.

By no means am I rallying a war against the press, but I hope for a pause for many in the industry to examine propaganda, agendas, political views, and the perception that we are at war in America. It is sort of an abstract civil war, but it is still a well-defined war that consists of conservatives versus liberals.

Narratives are the weapons and strategies of choice to saves lives. Even the Avengers faced a threat of politics in *Captain America: Civil War*. With many people fearing the actions of superheroes, the government decided to push for the Hero Registration Act, a law that limited a hero's activities. This results in a division in the Avengers. Iron Man stood with this act, claiming that their actions must be kept in check; otherwise, cities would continue to be destroyed. Captain America felt that saving the world was daring enough and that they could not rely on the government to protect the planet. This escalates into an all-out war between Team Iron Man (Iron Man, Black Panther, Vision, Black Widow, War Machine, and Spider-Man) and Team Captain America (Captain America, Bucky Barnes, Falcon, Scarlet Witch, Hawkeye, and Ant-Man) while a new villain emerges.

When politicians and world leaders think that people like Captain America and Iron Man are running amok, they tell them they need to be regulated. Tony Stark, Iron Man, thinks it's necessary. Steve Rogers, Captain America, doesn't think so. That eventually splits the Avengers.

At a UN gathering where the regulations were being worked out, an explosion killed some people, including the king of Wakanda. An investigation revealed that the bomb was planted by the Winter Soldier, Bucky Barnes, who was Captain America's friend during the war. Everyone wanted to get Barnes and kill him if necessary, but Steve wanted to get to him first and help him.

When Steve found him, Barnes said he didn't plant the bomb, and suddenly another person showed up all dressed in black. When the security forces caught up to them, they were arrested—and the one in black was revealed to be the son of the Wakanda king, T'Challa. The Black Panther was the guardian of Wakanda. While in custody, a psychiatrist was sent to evaluate Bucky, but when the power went out, he said some words to influence Bucky.

Bucky broke out, and Steve tried to get him. Believing that Bucky was innocent, Steve set out to find the man who got to him. Tony was also wanted because Steve helped Bucky. He asked War Machine and Black Widow to join him. He recruited someone to help him, and Widow asked T'Challa to join them. Steve brought Falcon with him, who got Ant-Man, and Steve called Hawkeye, who got Wanda, whom Tony has under lock and key under the eye of Vision. They got away, and Vision joined Tony. Eventually, they all had a confrontation.

Not even superheroes are free from agendas and narratives from politicians. Their perceptions become reality, and the storylines are being scripted into some of today's most popular movies. There was a *Fire Starter* involved, there were also *Flame Fanners*, and then there was the *Public*. If there were more *First Responders*, this possibly would not have happened. Either we are training our kids for the future—or we have begun to enjoy the drama that comes with fake news.

Political propaganda and narratives were not much of a threat to our society until nationally known broadcasters became fully committed to one agenda and one propaganda. This committed effort has confused Americans to the point they are disliking people they used to like. An American citizen has the right to choose (freedom). Do we believe that the professionals involved with nationally known stations do not understand or have crafty ways to drive the narratives they are employed by? I am sure the answer here is a resounding yes.

I believe wisdom doesn't share its beauty with narratives and agendas. It understands how the intelligent isolation of and from media propaganda is an essential qualification of the wise. I have lived uncommitted to any political side. I try at best to be thought of as Christian and not Evangelical. I am a "love thy neighbor" Christian—even thy neighbors in a foreign land.

The term "evangelical" comes from the Greek word for "gospel." The word comes from the Greek word "evangelion," which means good news or gospel. Historians believe that William Tyndale, a leader in the Protestant Reformation, was the first to record the English word "evangelical." In 1531, Tyndale wrote in a commentary on the book of John: "He exhorted them to proceed constantly in the evangelical truth." Later, the word was used by Catholic Sir Thomas More to describe Tyndale and his "evangelical brother (Robert) Barnes." Barnes was an English reformer. According to the Institute for the Study of American Evangelicals at Wheaton College, Martin Luther first used the Latinized form of the word *Evangelium* to describe the non-Catholic churches that came out of the Protestant Reformation.

Now that we understand Evangelism and its power in driving votes in America with a political agenda, propaganda, and narrative, do Christians have an allegiance to politics? Of course, one could debate that it was politics that got Jesus to the cross. If a Christian chooses a side, is that the only side going to heaven— or can individuals from either side go to heaven? If either side can go to heaven, then what are our arguments about then if not salvation issues between us.

As you can see, the waters begin to become very murky. I believe that Christ would choose no side because his focus was the needy, the faithful, and those who responded to the Gospel message. I believe the text reads "whosoever" in the Gospel.

In these troubling times, a man might use his faith to declare his belief in antiabortion and declare that no one who supports abortions is Christian because abortions are murder. Then Christ says to love thy neighbor and treat those in a foreign land with kindness, and this is no longer on the table as an identifier of Christians—just the antiabortion Christians.

Was it not Christ who said that they would know you are Christians by your love for one another? By no means am I supporting abortion, but I am shining a light on something Christ said he hated: hypocrisy.

Christians and Evangelicals have great power by being able to pray to God and ask for his blessings, and we are also responsible for those who stumble due to our actions. What does God have to say about this? I often say, "A child in the womb is no greater than the child in the room." It will not matter to Christ if they were here illegally or legally; he would care for the illegal as much as the legal and as he would care for the unborn child as much as the child in a cage in a room separated from their parents. If we are just pushing propaganda, narrative, and agenda, then are we sincere about abortions? What message have we sent if we do not respond to the persons who are being treated with the contention that were not aborted? Does that water down the point?

We can consider American, French, British, Christian, and pop culture. There is a world of understanding that the measure of responsibility is relative to the measure of power. Responsibility and power together seem great but harmless. We know that power by itself can be of great desire.

The ego is the component that can cause one to lose sight of the responsibility that comes with power. It may be more accurate to say that the superego is a more significant threat than the ego. The superego is not always responsible and is self-serving. When someone gains power, they must be careful and wise not to allow ego to drive that power. The superego is like an anesthesia that numbs the pain of stupidity.

America has a great richness about its current place. A capitalistic society has stated you can achieve what you are willing to sacrifice for. The playing field may not be fair, and some even have an advantage, but no one is short on opportunities to achieve. The NFL's New Orleans Saints have had three years of game-affecting calls not going their way, that caused them to lose in the playoffs. When asked why the calls were not overturned after the review on the replay, the answer was that there was still time on the clock for the New Orleans Saints to overcome those bad calls—maybe not all three times and maybe not the best reference for this point. I apologize.

The cards may be stacked against one person, but for the same scenario, another has shown that one can achieve great things with desire and focus. America has created multitudes of self-made millionaires. These individuals refused to fall to circumstances and decided to conquer events.

As we conquer and achieve, do we have any obligations? Did we achieve on our own? What makes a person great is when they decide to do for someone who cannot repay them. This impact goes on for lifetimes since the individual who was granted the gift begins to give and testify about the good experience. America became great by giving. Make no mistake about it—our giving is our greatness. With the power that America possesses, we have always chosen to be responsible in the world and not allow the ego to rule our power.

One area of giving for America is that of opportunity. America has offered open opportunities to the world. One could come to America and work hard and achieve. Through this achievement, immigrants could provide for their families, leave an inheritance to their children, and live the American dream. Today, the greatest thing we can provide to a person has become the greatest threat to America. America has been inundated with immigrants—and maybe more than we can serve.

The subject of this chapter is great power and great responsibility. Being responsible does not always feel good, and at times, it requires responsibility to make callous decisions. These decisions must be made without the use of feelings to ensure they are pure and intrinsic to protect the American public and our way of life.

This brings us to an important part of the problems in America. America has been the most popular destination for immigrants since the early 1960s, with one-fifth of the world's immigrants living here as of 2017. Despite its long history of immigration, America has juggled the pros and cons of immigration. At times, the diversity of America has been its greatest asset, and in other moments, it's been a fear that we cannot support everyone at this rate and not have a negative impact on those who are here legally or natively by birth.

In the most recent election, there has been a direct focus on immigration by Donald J. Trump and his administration. The perception is that this forward action toward addressing immigration is a direct attack on race more than a concern for the protection of the American public. One political party has also used this perception to advance political support in this regard of protecting people who can otherwise not defend themselves, immigrants, which is a very noble gesture if it is sincere and authentic.

Let us pause for a moment and consider the statistics on this subject. One does not have to be a supporter of the president in America. If you are a Christian, then we are required to honor the emperor or the president. 1 Peter 2:17 **NIV**. [17]Show proper respect to everyone, love the family of believers, fear God, honor the emperor. As Christians we should never bad-mouth the President, but honor him. We are to honor him because God commands us to, not because we deem him worthy of honor. Peter told his readers to honor the emperor, who was Nero, a wicked murderer. I am a respecter of our current president Donald Trump and Joe Biden, and I will show honor towards him or them by faith and by biblical sound doctrine. This posture towards the president is God's will. Many Christians and Evangelicals lost sight of this biblical standard during the Obama presidency, which caused others to reciprocate these actions towards our current administration. We should not allow this standard of dis-honoring the president to continue in our Christian walk.

The primary concern wrapped around immigration is closely related to discussions about the US economy, global competitiveness, national security, and the country's role in humanitarian giving and protection at a time of record global displacement. More than 43.7 million immigrants resided in the United States in 2016, accounting for 13.5 percent of the total US population of 323.1 million, according to the American Community Survey (ACS) data. Between 2015 and 2016, the foreign-born population increased by about 449,000, or 1 percent, a rate slower than the 2.1 percent growth experienced between 2014 and 2015 (1 Migration Policy Institute).

Immigrants and their American-born children now number approximately 86.4 million people, or 27 percent of the overall US population, according to the 2017 Current Population Survey (CPS). Amid these public debates and conversations, an informed general discussion upgrades and aids us in understanding, and in many cases, knowledge can bring peace to the open-minded and contrite in heart toward a solution.

The research being presented here offers a resource into the truth of the most current data available about the nearly 44 million immigrants living in America as of 2016. Many times, these heated debates and discussions do not have the answers to the most critical questions that determine the impact of the current momentum of immigration growth in America:

- ➤ How many people have immigrated to the United States?
- ➤ What channels are they coming in from?
- ➤ How many entered as refugees—and from which countries?
- ➤ Is Mexico still the top country of origin?
- ➤ Has the number of unauthorized immigrants changed in recent years?
- ➤ What jobs do immigrants tend to hold in the US labor market?
- ➤ How many US residents are immigrants or children of immigrants?

Let us define some of these questions to be better informed. As of 2016, 1.49 million foreign-born individuals moved to the United States, a 7 percent increase from the 1.38 million coming in 2015. India was the leading country of origin, with 175,100 arriving in 2016, followed by 160,200 from China/Hong Kong, 150,400 from Mexico, 54,700 from Cuba, and 46,600 from the Philippines. India and China surpassed Mexico in 2013 as the top origin countries for recent arrivals.

Among the top countries of recent immigrants, many more Cuban-born immigrants arrived in 2016 (54,700) than in 2015 (31,500)—an increase of 74 percent. In contrast, Canadian arrivals dropped 19 percent: 38,400 in 2016 versus 47,300 in 2015 (1 Migration Policy Institute).

While most of these arrivals are new to the United States, some may have previously resided in the country. Newly arrived immigrants are defined here as foreign-born individuals (ages one and older) who resided abroad one year prior to the survey, including naturalized citizens, lawful permanent residents, others who might have lived in the United States for some time prior to 2016, and temporary nonimmigrants and unauthorized immigrants (1 Migration Policy Institute).

I love the opportunities that America has provided for immigrants, refugees, and migrants. I support them. I also know and understand that we are at a point where we must examine the impact it has had beyond the positives to ensure America will not be negatively affected by the momentum of immigrants moving to America. We must collectively research this and decide if we need to do anything to care for this area. With great power comes great responsibility.

We must be responsible for what has made America great. I believe there is a way this concern can be handled with tact—where its tone is not misread into an aggressive approach to race. Just as one political party uses this current administration's posture toward immigration to draw in support of racism, the other political party is using the tone to draw in support from racists. Both political parties know the concerns, but the battle is about supporters and not about resolve first. Our political parties have failed us in one central area—and that is supporters over everything and supporters at all costs to win a position. We have taken on a strategy here, at the risk of over accomplishing steadfast resolve in America. Americans must choose to be informed first—think "we" and "one team" America—and decide unbiased politically to help in the healing of America. What role will you play?

What does God have to say?

> But the one who does not know and does things deserving punishment will be beaten with few blows. From everyone who has been given much, much will be demanded; and from the one who has been entrusted with much, much more will be asked. (Luke: 12:48)

In addition to what was captured in the Gospel of Luke, one might agree that a great demonstration of power and responsibility was delivered when Solomon asked for wisdom from God instead of conquering all his enemies. Solomon is described in the following favorable terms:

> Solomon loved the Lord, walking in the statutes of David, his father. (1 Kings 3:3 NIV)

> One night, the Lord appeared to Solomon and said, "Ask what I shall give you." (1 Kings 3:5 NIV)

> In response, Solomon answered, "Give your servant, therefore, an understanding mind to govern your people, that I may discern between good and evil, for who is able to govern this your great people?" (1 Kings 3:9 NIV)

> It pleased the Lord that Solomon had asked this. (1 Kings 3:10 NIV)

> God delights to give wisdom to those who truly seek it (Proverbs 2:6–8 NIV; James 1:5 NIV).

God responds to Solomon's request for wisdom by promising three different gifts. The first is the wisdom Solomon had asked for:

I now do according to your word. Behold, I give you a wise
and discerning mind so that none like you has been before
you and none like you shall arise after you. (1 Kings 3:12)

Don't be conformed to this world, but be transformed by
the renewing of your mind, so that you may prove what
is the ... the perfect will of God. (Romans 12:2 NIV)

In matters of civil obedience, Paul's advice was practical:
Don't call attention to yourself. Don't cause trouble. Pay
your taxes. Obey the law. Keep your nose clean. As he said
to the Romans, "Rulers are not a terror to the good work,
but to the evil." (Romans 13:3 NIV)

Peter's first letter told us to honor the emperor (the president).

Submit yourselves for the Lord's sake to every human
authority: whether to the emperor, as the supreme
authority, or to governors, who are sent by him to punish
those who do wrong and to commend those who do right.
For it is God's will that by doing good you should silence
the ignorant talk of foolish people. Live as free people,
but do not use your freedom as a cover-up for evil; live as
God's slaves. Show proper respect to everyone, love the
family of believers, fear God, honor the emperor. (1 Peter
2:13–17 NIV)

The bad news is that there are no perfect rulers, and there is no perfect
system of government. The good news is that this need not hinder us
from being faithful. In the Bible, a scapegoat is an animal that is ritually
burdened with the sins of others and then driven away. The concept first
appears in Leviticus, in which a goat is designated to be cast into the desert
to carry away the sins of the community.

In Christianity, this process prefigures the sacrifice of Christ on the
cross through which God has been propitiated, and sins can be expiated.
Jesus Christ is seen to have fulfilled all the biblical types: the high priest

who officiates at the ceremony, the Lord's goat that deals with the pollution of sin, and the scapegoat that removes the burden of sin.

Christians believe that sinners who own their guilt and confess their sins—exercising faith and trust in the person and sacrifice of Jesus—are forgiven of their sins. Since the second goat was sent away to perish, the word "scapegoat" has developed to indicate a person who is blamed and punished for the sins of others. In many cases, our leaders are blamed for our own sins. Christ was declared a perfect being and was still blamed for our sins. Hopefully we can forgive the sins of the forefathers of America since they need it as much as we do.

THREE

PERCEPTION
IS REALITY

Is perception reality? In 2008, while working in an AT&T call center, I was struggling with harmony on my team of associates. My boss was aware that my intentions were great, but it was troubling to understand the opposition on my team towards me.

I was the type of manager who would buy doughnuts for my team about two Mondays each month. I personalized many of the doughnuts in a mixed fashion. For example, one associate liked chocolate-filled doughnuts, one liked Bavarian crème-filled doughnuts, one liked cake doughnuts with icing, and others just enjoyed plain glazed doughnuts from America's best doughnut shop: Shipley's Donuts.

I also would cook a full-course meal for my team to celebrate any sales incentives that we achieved for the month. I would cook smothered steak, cornbread dressing, rolls, sides, and dessert. My team often raved about these feasts at the end of the month, but I still had enormous opposition from my team at work.

In 2008, a coworker, Rod Guillory, asked me to ride with him to run some errands during lunchtime. I said okay, and Rod said we would grab a bite to eat from a fast-food spot on the way back. During the ride, Rod asked about the relationships on my team and how it all was going. I explained what was taking place and the challenges with day-to-day resistance on action items within the team and how the items quickly escalated into contentious debates on the floor.

After I shared most of this with him, Rod said, "Perception is reality."

I said, "I do not agree with that. Perception is not reality."

Rod said, "What it means is that for others—your peers, subordinates, or superiors—how they perceive you is a reality for them. How you perceive yourself has nothing to do with it. It means that your behaviors and their results matter infinitely more than your intentions."

Perception is defined as the organization, identification, and interpretation of sensory information in order to represent and understand the environment. All perception involves signals in the nervous system, which result from physical or chemical stimulation of the sense organs.

Rod Guillory explained that my team was not judging me, reacting to me, or treating me based on the nice gestures, gifts, treats, or things I did for them, which was the reality of it all. They were responding to me based on their perceptions of me.

Rod said, "What is their perception of you?"

After Rod's careful definition and breakdown of perception, I knew that my answer could not be what I had just shared with him about reality.

I thought I should be honest about it all. I truly desired to get past this issue on my team and resolve it.

I said, "I believe that their perception of me is that I am arrogant, cold, short, and mean."

Rod asked, "Why would you say that?"

I said, "I know that I come across arrogant and cold because I had done one of these communication profiles surveys with the lion, otter, beaver, and golden retriever, and my survey came back as the lion. In the personality communication about the lion, it declared that the way I communicate is dominant, efficient, and straightforward. There was only one other lion personality on the team, and most of my team had beaver or otter personalities."

My team's perception of me was how they treated me and how they responded to me. If I wanted to change that relationship and be more effective in communicating with them, I had to help change that perception.

Rod was giving me encouragement. It was starting to make sense to me. I could see the point he was making, and I must admit, at the start of this conversation, I was almost 100 percent sure he was totally wrong in what he was saying to me.

When I got back to work, I began to work on changing the perception—and I even saved money in the process. I didn't have to buy all those good doughnuts on Mondays, and I didn't have to cook those huge meals for my team if I could change their perception of me. I began to listen more, show more empathy, support them more when they were frustrated with a process, and be in tune with their feelings and needs each day. It took about six months, but I saw a transition to minimum resistance. I had been fighting a battle I would never win.

Imagine if everyone did a self-examination of the perceptions of themselves by family members, coworkers, and friends. What if our government did a self-reflection of perception of themselves by the public and decided to address just a few of those perceptions? How powerful would that be? What if the president addressed some of the perceptions about himself to the public? Would it help? Would it show weakness? Perception is strong and becomes that individual's reality.

Black Lives Matter

Death has a way of encouraging thoughts to desire contentment and a replay in the mind of fond memories. For example, Death can cause the events that lead one towards gratitude, that they survived an event that others were not as fortunate. Death can also cause a pause to listen to the pain that was behind the tragedy before it happened. It was Jesus's death on the cross that placed a sense of urgency in the disciples to now lead and evangelize. They no longer had the benefit of relying on Christ to do the works, that he had now given them the talents for. His death reminded them. His resurrection convicted them. Death played an important role in this pivotal moment of faith. Today from a death, what can we learn? What can we do differently to avoid another tragedy of death? What urgency did it now place in us as Americans?

Death can also spawn the violence and vengeance needed to evoke change in matters that have not changed. In this country, many are "nobodies" until "somebody" kills them (Notorious B.I.G.). In each case, significant pivots in America came after substantial bloodshed. Spiritually, we did not pivot until Jesus Christ was sacrificed. It was in the blood that was shed for the remission of our sins that we begin to pivot or repent and turn away from sin.

It has been argued that George Floyd was no martyr or pivoting point in America. Could George Floyd be the pivotal point in America for change? Was it not Rosa Parks that spawned the Civil Rights Movement? Rosa Parks broke the law by refusing to give up her seat on a public bus, to a White Man, and move further to the back of the bus. This posture taken by Rosa Parks drew the attention needed to address a growing issue in America. Is George Floyd a modern day Rosa Parks? I guess if we judge him and shame his track record we remove that convincing conclusion, but if we considered the attention this loss of life brought to the awareness of the growing issue of Police Brutality then we would have to consider George Floyd's death as a pivotal moment in this hot topic. George Floyd, mass shootings in schools, Native Americans, African American slaves, the Civil War, Pearl Harbor, Martin Luther King, John F. Kennedy, and even to save the world, blood had to be shed. I say this not to excuse or encourage bloodshed, but to ask, "*Is there a sacrificial message to it for significant change to finally happen?"* Even Abraham in the Bible was asked to shed the blood of his son for the original promise we all inherit by giving our lives to Christ. Is it of God to gain our attention in those moments and pivot and turn away (repent)? Are we also given a ram in the bush in those moments? Are we also given an alternative sacrifice to send the same message and retrieve the same promise or change?

Is the Black Lives Matter movement driven by perception or reality? It really doesn't matter if it is a true reality (though it is) because we have already seen the reactions to the public outcry. Many Americans' perception is that this is a reality that they must declare that their own lives matter.

I have often thought that *"matter"* is the lowest form of value being requested here, and even that request has offended some people. It is just a simple request to say "they matter" and that "they count." Not that they are more important or greater, dominant, but simply that "they matter." This is not a big request. Can we agree that we all matter?

What is the response by many? "All lives matter!" For "all lives matter" to be a valid statement, then Black lives must matter or count. There is some difficulty for some people to agree that just saying that Black lives matter is a true statement. Pride maybe? Pride is a sin, and God hates it. I think logically we must agree on that.

We should have enough humility in our hearts to say Black lives matter without feeling a need to defend our own value if we are of another race. Suggesting that Black is included in all should help the narrowest minded individual get on board. Simple math is that *all* includes *Black*.

Pride comes before destruction and does not heal. It continues to harm open wounds. The Black Lives Matter statement becomes someone else's perception of a threat. It doesn't matter if it is a fact or not. By their perception, that is their reality.

Since BLM drives perception as well and is also being utilized by leftist political agendas to gain voters, it removes the merits of the genuine interest to protect the unarmed public. You are not considering me, you are placing yourself above me, or you see me now as less important are not exactly the feelings of the opposition. It is simply to counter the political agendas.

We are living in a severely *"Partisan"* America. Seventy plus million on either side accounted for and more that didn't vote. We have a severely "Partisan" Media, Government, and Judiciary. Severely "Partisan" arrangements do not allow for sincerity or genuine postures, but yet postures that are more discipline and strategic to the "Party's" interest. This strategy of planting confusion, judgment, and categorizing man, are not of God. They are divisions planted by Satan. In his craftiness he convinces each side they are ultimately right and accurate to the point that they can justify their sins towards one another by believing they are morally required to do so. You want to know the recipe for war? Well it was just spelled out. Men and Women must be courageous enough to come out of the "Partisan" trenches. Hands up in humility and say let's work together. We must have leadership willing to showcase humility towards one another as the first example. There is "Ending" and then there is "Mending". Mending is a mutual middle to not end but agree in partial to move forward in peace. One very strong Christian pillar is that of forgiveness. We must in America be willing to "Forgive". We must forgive Donald Trump. We must forgive Joe Biden. We must forgive Kamala Harris. We must forgive Mike Pence. We must forgive the right. We must forgive the Left. We must forgive family members. We must forgive co-workers. We must forgive Facebook followers of opposing views. We must forgive politicians.

"America, we must forgive one another."

Once a Christian forgives, Satan has lost the war. Satan can keep his small victories, but the "war" is over. Much of what we need to forgive is based on a "Perception" and not a true reality. Yet this is not to minimize that it has become that person's reality, regardless. Perception is often the enemy. We must be alert. Are my feelings based on "Perception"? We must be able to answer that. More than likely that answer will often be yes. Addressing perceptions is not the responsibility of owner, but in most cases, it is the responsibility of the protagonist of those perceptions. I could not go to my team and say, "well that's just your perception of me" and hold no ownership of it. If I wanted to be effective as a leader and work in harmony, I had to be humble and address the perceptions without them even knowing the strategy. This strategy took time. I had to just go day by day doing a little more to address the perceptions.

Police in America will have to eventually address perceptions in the areas they serve in. Politicians will have to begin to address perceptions and not stay disciplined to partisan postures if we are to heal in America. Our President will have to understand "Perceptions" and work towards keeping them at the forefront of his approach to each situation he addresses.

Mr. President ~ Consider these 2 questions before responding

Do I understand the "Culture" involved?
Do I understand the "Perception" involved?

Let's examine some highly partisan issues and the perceptions that come along with them. I know this will be uncomfortable for some, but it is necessary to grow. I have seen many declare that Black lives matter with a preface to explain they are not trying to be offensive. If we are to heal, we must consider how much of the perception is reality. An understanding here can help heal and caution us on the response we may give. Check if their pain is present. If it is, then have empathy. Observe and realize there is just an evil present. If so, then ignore it.

We must respond to each scenario on an individual basis to draw an excellent conclusion from what we are observing in tone, body language, and context. Self-examine. Can my response help to heal or harm further? Define it. If you can identify the perception, you can adjust to help progress the relationship. Gaining the relationship is the ultimate goal in helping America heal. Relationships are a must, and in many cases, simple perceptions harm people from advancing in their relationships. If we take some extra care in our response and approach, we can help each other heal.

In May 2020, George Floyd was arrested in Minneapolis for exchanging a counterfeit twenty-dollar bill, and the arresting police officer used excessive force. The perception here was that an officer showed little value for the Black man's life. He was pleading with the officers to let him breathe and to not kill him. Three officers held George Floyd down for nearly nine minutes with extreme pressure on several parts of his body, disrupting his ability to breathe. As a result, George Floyd died. One of the officers showed extreme negligence by placing a knee on George Floyd's neck until he died. It was a standard arrest, but it was not a standard procedure in the arrest to place knee on the neck of a suspect.

Closer examination makes the situation look like a calculated hit or premeditated intent to kill George Floyd. If it were calculated and an actual assigned hit, then was race the motivation? The public saw something so hurtful that it responded to its initial perceptions. This is not to say the perceptions were not truths. This is just one of several situations where a White cop killed an unarmed Black man in the last ten years. That simple statement is true, but the story behind it is what we are trying to understand. Perception does not care about the story behind it because it already has its reality. Perception is powerful and drives behaviors, responses, and decisions. This investigation into the George Floyd case is to be determined, but I want to share what this perception has accomplished thus far.

So, what has perceptions and protests accomplished? Did the protests harm or advance the cause? Different people may have different perceptions of the protests.

- Minneapolis banned the use of chokeholds.
- Charges were upgraded against Officer Chauvin, and his accomplices were arrested and charged.
- Dallas adopted a "duty to intervene" rule that requires officers to stop other cops who are engaging in inappropriate use of force.
- New Jersey's attorney general said the state would update its use-of-force guidelines for the first time in two decades.
- In Maryland, a bipartisan workgroup of state lawmakers announced a police reform work group.
- The Los Angeles City Council introduced a motion to reduce LAPD's $1.8 billion operating budget.
- The MBTA in Boston agreed to stop using public buses to transport police officers to protests.
- Police brutality captured on cameras led to near-immediate suspensions and firings of officers in several cities, including Buffalo and Fort Lauderdale.
- Monuments celebrating confederate soldiers were removed in Virginia, Alabama, and other states.
- The street in front of the White House was renamed "Black Lives Matter Plaza."
- Military forces began to withdraw from Washington.

Then, there's all the other stuff that's hard to measure:

- Difficult public and private conversations about race and privilege started to happen.
- Some White people started talking about racism and the role of policing in this country.
- Internal battles started exploding within organizations over issues that had been simmering or ignored for a long time. Some organizations would end as a result; others would be forever changed or replaced with something more robust and fairer.

- Protests against racial inequality sparked by the police killing of George Floyd started taking place all over the world.
- Rallies and memorials have been held in cities across Europe, as well as in Mexico, Canada, Brazil, Australia, and New Zealand.
- As the United States contended with its second week of protests, issues of racism, police brutality, and oppression were brought to light across the globe.
- "People all over the world understand that their own fights for human rights, for equality and fairness, will become so much more difficult to win if we are going to lose America as the place where 'I have a dream' is a real and universal political program," Wolfgang Schwinger, a former German ambassador to the United States, told the *New Yorker*.
- In France, protesters marched holding signs that said "I can't breathe" to signify both the words of Floyd and the last words of Adama Traore, a twenty-four-year-old Black man who was subdued by police officers outside of Paris in 2016. Traore gasped the sentence before he died.
- In Amsterdam, an estimated ten thousand people filled the Dam Square holding signs and shouting popular chants like "Black lives matter" and "No justice, no peace."
- In Germany, people gathered in multiple locations throughout Berlin to demand justice for Floyd and to fight against police brutality.
- A mural dedicated to Floyd was also spray-painted on a stretch of wall in Berlin that once divided the German capital during the Cold War.
- In Ireland, protesters held a peaceful demonstration outside of Belfast's city hall, and others gathered outside of the American embassy in Dublin.
- In Italy, protesters gathered and marched with signs: "Stop killing Black people," "Say his name," and "We will not be silent."
- In Spain, people gathered to march and hold up signs throughout Barcelona and Madrid.
- In Athens, Greece, protesters took to the streets to collectively hold up a sign that read "I can't breathe."

- In Brussels, protesters were sitting in a peaceful demonstration in front of an opera house in the center of the city.
- In Denmark, protesters were heard chanting, "No justice, no peace!" throughout the streets of Copenhagen, and others gathered outside the American embassy.
- In Canada, protesters were also grieving for Regis Kochanski-Paquet, a twenty-nine-year-old Black woman who died after falling from her balcony during a police investigation in her building.
- In New Zealand, roughly two thousand people marched to the American embassy in Auckland, chanting and carrying signs demanding justice.
- Memorials have been built for Floyd around the world, too. In Mexico City, portraits of him were hung outside the American embassy with roses, candles, and signs.
- In Poland, candles and flowers were laid out next to photos of Floyd outside the American consulate.
- In Syria, two artists created a mural depicting Floyd in the northwestern town of Binnish, "on a wall destroyed by military planes."

Perception Becomes Reality

Journey out to the southwest desert, and catch one hundred red fire ants, as well as one hundred large black ants, and place them all in a jar together, you will find at first, nothing will happen. Then if you violently shake the jar, and then dump them back on the ground the ants will start to fight each other until they eventually kill each other. The shaking of the jar creates confusion and chaos, and the red ants begin to believe they are under attack by the black ants. The black also begin to believe they are under attack by the red ants. Who is the real enemy? I will say it again. There was a *Fire Starter* involved, there were also a *Flame Fanner*, and then there was the *Public*. If there were more *First Responders*, this possibly would not have happened. Even with Ants.

Initially the enemy is the person shaking the jar, but once the fighting starts the enemies become who is attacking you now, with no real threat present. In our current times in America we have many "Jar Shakers". In many cases these are the social media gas lighters, media political broadcast organizations, and or political podcast. What if you could identify every political flame fanner on your Facebook network of friends and then begin to delete them one by one. How do you think your mental health would be impacted? These individuals are convinced they are making a difference. More harm than good.

Today Liberal vs Conservative, Black vs White, Pro Mask vs Anti Mask, etc. The real question we need to be asking ourselves is who is shaking the jar and why? Then step two is to tell everyone to stand down, there is no real threat here. All perception. We should be able to communicate on all fronts and platforms without feeling threatened or the need to avenge our positions. Just listening helps us to heal, with no response other than something empathetic. Perceptions must be addressed in the healing process. Trust cannot be gained without addressing the perception. Today Conservatives have mixed feelings about the outcome of this Election, and they have perceptions about how the victory was accomplished. To shame the loser is not the answer.

One contrary perception to the above Black Lives Matter movement is the Sheriff David Clarke for US Senate draft committee that says Black Lives Matter is a terrorist movement and a hate group. They call it "Black *Lies* Matter." Clarke has repeatedly used *lies* instead of *lives* in labeling the group and has frequently called it a hate group. This is mainly due to its founding members having Marxist influences. By title, it appeals to one group, and by mission statement, it is detested by another. In his memoir, he called the group a "terrorist organization." He believes this movement is minimizing the officers' ability to do their jobs safely and to protect the public.

Hawk Newsome, a regional president of the Black Lives Matter movement, has a totally different perception of his organization and his personal intent. This is not to say that Hawk agrees with the full mission statement of the movement, but he has a genuine interest in doing a better job of protecting unarmed Black men from excessive and lethal force of the police. How can these two well-educated individuals be so far from common ground? Each person has a different perception of the organization, and in their personal worlds, it is a reality.

David Clarke is a Police Officer. Hawk Newsome is an activist. These two worlds are in natural opposition to each other. Who is wrong? Could they both be right? It would be almost impossible to reduce the distance of disagreement between these two individuals due to the dedication and fiduciary duty they both feel. I would like to submit these two individuals for the Social Lunch Challenge in Section 4. I would like to submit Candance Owens and Angela Rye for the Social Lunch Challenge. I would like to offer the president of the United States and Collin Kaepernick for the Social Lunch Challenge. Some of these are extreme, but wouldn't the nation like to see some of these American Citizens partake in a peaceful sit-down meal to discuss a few things? There is only one way to mend the disagreements, and that is to reduce or eliminate the distrust between the two oppositions. This only happens through an intrinsic growth in the potential relationship between them. This is where it starts with us commoners. Spend time with some people with opposing views—and open your heart and mind to gain common ground. Part of the healing process will be finding common ground. Perception is reality. Perception becomes a reality for the most unique relationships and on certain topics. What people perceive about a particular issue or person becomes their reality.

Political parties have used perception to aid their narrative strategies, which should be considered an Integrity challenge. In many cases, politicians know the truth, but they play on the perceptions to gain support because the perception is a stronger strategy than the truth.

The Media and Political Parties understand there is a *Fire Starter* involved, there are also *Flame Fanners*, and then there was the *Public*. If there were more *First Responders*, this possibly would not have happened. The media and political parties know they have "Flame Fanners" out in the field ready to work at a moment's notice on submission of their information. Some of them are famous for their political views and others are just normal citizens that are bored on social media and desperately seeking to be relatable.

Media and Political Activists understand the meaning of working the perceptions will be more effective for gaining the support and voters on certain topics and for certain candidates. This is what I learned as well with my AT&T team, which I mentioned in the preface. Their perception of me was stronger than the truth about me. If I wanted to change the relationship between us, I had to swallow my pride, be humble, and focus on the perception. Once I addressed the perception, I could rework the truth.

A true and intrinsic resolve here is to help perception and truth match up. We must work at understanding the perception and use humility and careful adjustment to bring the perception up to what is true. The person wholeheartedly believes in the perception and reacts to it like any other natural survival mechanism we have built into our psyches.

Perception and reality have a complicated relationship with each other. We cannot always perceive reality directly, but we are still able to interact with it and learn about it. In most cases, perception is all we have. Arguably some may say it is not possible to experience physical reality, meaning what is really "there," directly. With that said, we live inside the world of our perceptions. The brain does its best job that it can at keeping our perceptions consistent with what is truly real on the information it receives from the senses, and a short distance between perception and reality consistency is ultimately the best we can hope for.

While this entire process is rolling out, one's perceptual system is constructed so that what we can experience what feels like a proper physical reality. When people learn to draw or paint, they must become aware of what they are perceiving as far as color, perspective, and shape—and often for the first time. The brain's translation from perception into a model of reality is so instinctive that we unaware it is happening, and it takes practice and training to become aware of it. This awareness includes all the errors and distortions that our perceptual processes routinely impose on our experiences, which can be revealed as an optical illusion.

In America today, much of our problem is caused by perceptions of what may or may not be real. If we are not well informed statistically about certain topics, then perception can be used to control our feelings and disposition about certain issues. Until others start the process of working to change the perception, it will be challenging to improve relationships in America and dissolve the tribal country we are becoming. The two tribes are the two political parties, and they are at war.

Here are some perceptions today. Keep in mind these are most likely not accurate, but for many, this is their perception, which makes it their reality:

- All Republicans are racist.
- All Democrats support abortions.
- Donald Trump has a race-driven agenda.
- All liberals support same-sex marriages and transgender equality.
- All gays are Democrats.
- The NRA does not care about lives.
- Cops shoot to kill Blacks more often than Whites.
- Blacks and Democrats do not value cops' lives.
- Obamacare was a win for Obama.

It is no secret that the media can influence the general public's opinion on almost anything. Whether the subject is fiction or nonfiction, movies, documentaries, and the news can sway the public's views and perceptions one way or the other. Not even the world of law enforcement is safe from the media's purview. Media portrayals often romanticize law enforcement as a well-oiled machine that always gets the bad guy and has a perfect relationship with the public. On top of this, the media has displayed a poor habit of portraying crime as predominantly violent and racially driven rather than showing the whole picture.

One of the largest ways the media influences public opinions is through the news. News outlets report on local and world events, often applying their own biases to advance their agendas. All these items drive behavior, responses, hard feelings, and emotions. The list above could be a thousand pages long. These topics have strong perceptions about them and severely manipulate discomfort and emotions. It is not that any of them are proven facts all the time, but due to their perceptions, they have a reality clause to them that drives behavior through perception. Whether they are factual or not, that is someone's new reality.

How do we positively change or affect perception? We must solve problems by identifying them. We must become aware and then agree that in the core problem is the true issue. I was able to change my relationship with my team at AT&T by focusing on their perceptions of me. It was a powerful strategy.

Once you know the perception, you have to begin to do the opposite— genuinely. Today, there is a movement of African-American conservatives who follow the traditional perceptions of the Republican Party, including

Candance Owens, CJ Pearson, the Hodgetwins, and Sheriff David Clarke. I have taken the time to watch and observe these individuals to gain knowledge of their positions and reasons for deciding to be Republicans. I have learned that I cannot disagree with many of their positions, but I have found myself disagreeing with how they have presented their cases. Perception becomes reality. Even though I can agree with them, I struggle with the perception.

Prager University and other platforms are engaged in this political space to peel back some of the perceptions, but in the process, they often begin painting new perceptions. Give each of these platforms a chance and an ear. Evaluate with integrity and see what happens. I encourage you to do this in the process of healing.

To successfully unravel perceptions, humility and sincere listening have to be included. I eventually agreed with Rod Guillory and went beyond popular belief and my initial instincts and psyche. Before we take on a posture, ask, "Is this my perception—or have I researched enough to know the truth?" Remember with great power comes great responsibility, and we all have a responsibility to research and know for sure before our dispositions are confirmed strictly by perception.

What does God have to say? Our perceptions are the lens that we view life with. Every thought, opinion, and experience is processed through our perceptions. Jesus said that if our eyes are healthy, then our whole bodies would be full of light (Matthew 6:23 NIV). The same is true for our perceptions. If our perceptions are healthy, then our entire lives will be filled with light or optimism. On the other hand, if our perceptions are unhealthy, then our lives become a dark place:

> Jesus also said, "If then the light within you is darkness, how great is that darkness!" (Matthew 6:23 NIV)

If we choose to see all that is wrong with ourselves, with others, or with anything else, we'll inevitably find it. If we can't find it, we'll create it. Our perceptions have the incredible power to shape our circumstances so they align with what we already believe. This is not a healthy exercise, and it often yields a lower quality of life:

The eye is the lamp of the body. If your eyes are healthy, your whole body will be full of light. But if your eyes are unhealthy, your whole body will be full of darkness. If then the light within you is darkness, how great is that darkness! "No one can serve two masters. Either you will hate the one and love the other, or you will be devoted to the one and despise the other. You cannot serve both God and money. (Matthew 6:22–24 NIV)

If we believe what the Bible says about perceptions, we must honestly examine them on a regular basis. Bad experiences and bad information result in faulty perceptions. Faulty perceptions lead to misdirection and disconnection. Let there be light in our perceptions so that we may see what is true and real.

Section One - Social Challenge

Restoring or re-enforcing a sense of pride in our country is important. 9/12/01 was a day All Americans unified and were ready to defend our land at any cost. This should always be our posture in America. Film and Post to Social Media a vacation you went on to see some historical sites in America. Share a demonstration of respect for that History with friends and family. Expand on what it means to be an American and do not leave out the dark truths and bright sides as well. Remember, dark truths build character. We must grow through what we have gone through in America. History is important; let's learn together. Point out what is real and how this History may have overall impacted Americans eventually in a positive way. Pressure must hit the coal before it yields a diamond. With more Americans sharing History, the sense of pride will start to educate and rebuke the powers against this great country. We must be sure this pride in America does not become idolized and is simply being shared to help each other grow in gratitude for our home, which is the USA.

SECTION II

THE CAUSE

FOUR

THE WAR ON CULTURE

In chapters 1–3, we identified the problems in America. The issues are just facts that would persist without any human involvement to push them. We will now entertain the causes.

The causes will be wrapped around the pushing of agendas by

Americans. In America, there is a war on culture. Culture is defined as the scenario of living developed by a social group and translated from one generation to another. In America, several cultures are under attack.

I have often tried to live in such a way to place myself in position to always prove stereotypes wrong. I try to understand what other races may perceive of the Black race and be sure to counter those stereotypes. For example, I try to be on time to work, on time to meetings, and on time to family events. I pride myself on being prepared and ready for anything I am involved in. As you can see, these are some of the stereotypes of African Americans. When I am at any restaurant, I tip 20 percent—even on lousy service. I might tip more on good service. I figure that I can affect perception by doing the opposite of what many believe about my race.

I believe one of the enemies of America today is the ideology of all— even when unstated. I do not believe that "all" white Americans have been privileged and had an advantage for their entire lives. It is simply not true. Many have worked hard and lived in modest ways like any other families in the United States. Many African Americans have been on time to their jobs and meetings for years, and many tip well. All cops are not bad cops looking for the next opportunity to perform police brutality.

All becomes an antagonist to the psyche. We must rise above the all. We must isolate people for who they really are and not categorize them by all. Many Democrats and African Americans respect the police, and many White Americans were not privileged growing up. Many worked hard to achieve what they have today for their families. With all that said, that doesn't mean these stereotypes are not accurate at times or that privilege doesn't exist. These areas are not perceptions; they are real.

Is there a war on White culture? The war is not on all White culture, but the White culture of White privilege. Some people see this as a good thing, and others feel threatened by it due to areas of comfort being dissolved and attacked daily.

What is White culture versus White privilege? White Americans are descendants of any of the White racial groups of Europe, the Middle East, and North Africa, or in census statistics, those who self-report as white based on having majority-white ancestry. The United States Census Bureau defines White people as those "having origins in any of the original peoples of Europe, the Middle East, or North Africa." That is probably a shocking statement.

Like in all the official US racial categories, White has a "non-Hispanic or Latino" and a "Hispanic or Latino" component, the latter consisting mostly of white Mexican Americans and White Cuban Americans. The term Caucasian is erroneously considered interchangeable with White, although the latter is used in the narrower sense of White-skinned. Increasingly non-European ethnic groups are traditionally identified as White by the US Census, such as Arab Americans, Jewish Americans, and Hispanics or Latinos who may not be considered or identified as White by some.

Within the United States, however, cultural pollination is a real item today. The primarily Irish, Italian, and German communities have dissipated into relatively undifferentiated Whiteness. American cultural groups, while more quickly identifiable, are being consistently affected.

From a broadly generalized view, cultural differences are becoming fewer and less pronounced. What were once culture-specific traditions and practices are now freely practiced by members of other cultural groups— even as they are rejected by some members of the cultural group that developed the practices initially placed out of a desire to let go of traditional ways and pop culture or "fit in" with the mainstream.

Demonstrations of privilege can be a choice. It can be a decision not to value or desire to understand culturally different groups—even when members of those groups are our neighbors, our coworkers, our children's classmates, and sometimes even our friends. Exercising modern-day acts of privilege can be a decision that any race researcher or activist will point out is available specifically to members of a majority group.

The company of racial minority groups, like members of other visible minority groups, must understand that the majority of culture to negotiate it with any degree of success. The real privilege of Whiteness is the ability to make decisions regarding which groups are worth listening to, when, and under what circumstances. This is a luxury of White privilege. These choices are so often taken for granted that many of us make it with hardly any awareness of doing anything at all. This decision making is stealthy and subconscious, and it is quickly suppressed.

For the past decade, it has been almost impossible to address in a clear structural manner—no matter how many writers and bloggers have written about it. The premise of this question was grounded in a conversation where someone suggested that White Americans were mere "borrowers" and "tinkerers" of the cultures of others rather than being original developers of anything solely their own. On the surface, this argument seemed to have merit. The more I pondered the topic, the more I was able to identify some cultural purities of the white American race. Here are a few examples of distinctly white American culture:

The invention of blue jeans was a contribution to the fashion we still take pride in America today. Arguably one of the most popular clothing articles of modern Western society, blue jeans can be attributed to white Americans.

- Cowboys. Although history buffs will argue that the cowboy concept was born in Spain, the modern perception of a cowboy is mostly a construct of White America.
- Driving. Driving as a means of common transportation is primarily a White American construct. America didn't invent the automobile, but it did develop the concept of everyday driving and traffic laws.
- Basketball. Although now dominated by African Americans, the game of basketball was originally a predominantly White sport. Basketball is one of the few sports that is not primarily an alteration of another sport.
- Hippies. White America created a complete subculture centered on the concepts of sex, drugs, activism, and universal peace.
- Racism. Whereas historical disenfranchisement of groups of people was primarily based on class and social status, White America propagated the disenfranchisement of people solely based on skin tone. Although slavery was neither new nor unique to America, the modern concept of racial superiority and inferiority is a construct of White America, and now it seems we own all history on slavery. We must understand this is not true. We own our history of slavery here in America, but we did not invent it.

Those are but a few examples. I hope they help you get your mental motors going.

Is this the end of traditional White culture in America? The answer is no, but is that a fear of many in the United States today and a perception that is driving fear and reaction? Yes is the answer. Fear is our top decision-making driver. Media and politicians are very aware of this psyche about people. They use this to their advantage to drive decision-making.

Taking down of all the confederate monuments is one culture saying, "Remove the memorializing of slave masters and/or White supremacy." For others, the perception is saying, "This is an attack on White America, and they will come for us next." If politicians and the media want to drive support, they drive fear. Pay attention to that as you watch the news and social media. Driving fear will drive support for your cause. How do we counter that? We do not get excited or start to fear based on perceptions. We learn and wait. We take control of our emotions. Fear owns our emotions, and most of our decision-making comes from this natural process.

The fear that drives systemic racism still needs to be addressed. The election of Barack Obama was the most startling manifestation of a larger trend· the gradual erosion of whiteness as the touchstone of what it means to be American.

If the end of White America is a cultural and demographic inevitability, what will the new mainstream look like? How will White Americans fit into it? What will it mean to be White when whiteness is no longer the norm? And will a post-white America be less racially divided—or more so? Will there be a natural human defense mode of preservation?

Consider White America is more than 50 percent of the population, and Black America is only 16 percent of the population. Do you feel that Black America is a threat to White America? By the numbers, no. The Hispanic and Asian populations are growing at a much faster rate and are a bigger threat if we are simply considering "fear factors."

Perception is powerful, and we have to stay aware of the drivers of perception. It is really evil to manipulate this without integrity, and it is harming the peace in America. Many will say that Donald Trump has come to preserve White culture and White privilege. Is this perception true? Let's not confirm if it's true or not but let us agree that this murmuring exists and is relevant in much of the current dialogues about race. On social networks, it has become a fear factor. This fear factor is being used to drive animosity toward the president. Is the president defending his culture? Does he recognize there is a war against his specific culture—or is that another fear factor? These questions should get our thoughts moving. I do not want to offend anyone, but knowing the enemy helps heal. The enemy in many cases is simple perceptions and fear factors, which are not necessarily legit threats.

In elementary school, Dr. Sanjay Gupta asked his mom if he could change his name to Steven so that he could fit in more at school. His mom asked him how many Stevens there were in his class, and he responded with six. His mom said if all those Stevens do good, then you will just blend in, or if they all do wrong, then you could get associated with them. Dr. Gupta's mom told him if he just would be Sanjay, he could earn his own merits at the right time. They went to sleep that night, and his mom told him she was going to sign the paperwork to have his name changed to Steven. Dr. Gupta told his mom that he wanted to keep his name. Dr. Gupta's mom placed in her son that day an identity and a perspective of that identity—and look at the results.

The harm that has affected Black Americans in the long term is the harsh hits on the African American identity. We addressed much of this with the story of Jane Elliott. Each race in America has had some sort of identity crises, and some have tried to address this challenge.

Many Asians and Indians have changed their names to American names at early ages. I have even seen CIOs and CEOs with two names listed on their signature lines. One is their American name, and the other is their given name. If you have become a medical doctor or a CIO, there is no longer a need to have to address the insecurities of your heritage or cultural name.

Many people are aware of the systemic racism that can come with having a culturally defined original name. Bill Imada, head of the I. W. Group, a prominent Asian American communication and marketing company, said "I think in the 1920s, 1930s, and 1940s, for anyone who immigrated, the aspiration was to blend in and be as American as possible so that White America wouldn't be intimidated by them. The intent was to imitate White America as much as possible. They would learn English, go to church, go to the same schools."

Whether you describe it as the dawning of a post-racial age or just the end of traditional White America, we are approaching a profound demographic pivot point. According to a US Census Bureau study conducted in 2008, the groups currently categorized as racial minorities—Blacks, Hispanics, East Asians, and South Asians—will account for most of the American population by 2042. Among Americans under the age of eighteen, this shift is projected to take place in 2023, which means that every child born in the United States from here on out will belong to the first post-white generation per this study.

Interracial marriage increasingly makes this picture more complex and less and less predictable. Considering the validity in what Michael Lind has described as the "beiging" of America, it may have traction. It is possible that "beige Americans" will self-identify as "White" in enough numbers to push the pivot point further into the future than the Census Bureau projects. Patrick Mahomes, the Super Bowl MVP 2020, Barack Obama the forty-fourth president of the United States, and Blake Griffin, prolific NBA All-Star, are just a few examples of this.

In America, are we still waiting for the time where we are judged more significantly by character? Is this not a person's essential quality and undisputedly the soundest standard of evaluation? Do our political parties judge by character or by agreement on the subject? Would God judge by works and fruit or by political agreement?

Christians often fall prey to this compromise while trying to be engaged citizens. I will say this again, As Christians, we forfeit the freedom of speech. We can only speak as to the oracles of God:

> If anyone speaks, they should do so as one who speaks the very words of God. If anyone serves, they should do so with the strength God provides, so that in all things God may be praised through Jesus Christ. To him be the glory and the power for ever and ever. Amen. (1 Peter 4:11 NIV)

We can only speak to build up or edify:

Do not let any unwholesome talk come out of your mouths, but only what is helpful for building others up according to their needs, that it may benefit those who listen. (Ephesians 4:29 NIV)

We are allotted freedom of speech—but only the speech the Bible supports. Any freedom or liberty of speech the Holy Spirit governs within us is the right discernment one should have. Christ would be interested in a person's character—and so shall Christians who have put on Christ.

When someone becomes a Christian, they give up freedom of speech. The First Amendment gives Americans the right to express any opinions without censorship or restraint. The Bible removes this freedom from us once we are baptized into Christ. Today, even social media platforms are removing these rights when they see harmful or misleading statements. We are so competitive in winning the political battles that content is no longer governed by the Spirit of God, but by the spirit the world gives to seek the victory in propaganda and minimize the priority of the public's well-being through the process.

Character is the most distinctive nature of a person. Let us reflect in the word's origins. Content, in this context, is what is held within or entirely inside. Character is what makes someone what he or she is. It includes what they believe in and how they behave. Are they honest, kind, friendly, loving, respectful, and so on? It is like personality.

Martin Luther King introduced this exercise of judgment and was really asking that people be judged by behavior rather than appearance. Biblically, this would be by their fruit and not the origin. Moral character or character is an evaluation of an individual's stable moral qualities.

The concept of character can imply a variety of attributes, including the existence or lack of virtues such as empathy, courage, fortitude, honesty, and loyalty—or of good behaviors or habits. Some qualities can dramatically improve the ethical quality of our decisions around our personal character and the character of others. Trustworthiness, respect, responsibility, fairness, caring, and citizenship are some areas to search for within ourselves and are the pillars of character.

In America, character is not required if we agree with the individual politically. Digest that for a moment. If you agree with a person politically, you are no longer required to agree with them morally. Is that not a truth today? We probably could write down a list of those who have been given what some may call White privilege in moral standards or simply political party privilege in moral standards and are exempt from being judged by the content of their character.

Americans have even accepted the notion that they get to judge character by how they feel about someone rather than getting to know them. Is this an intelligent approach? Does it have a healthy merit of yielding something positive if it is consistently used for a diagnosis about citizens in this country?

Christians can be guilty of these iniquities as well. We are subject to extreme perceptions about political figures without research, and peer pressure makes us side with our feelings rather than a clear evaluation of character. If deciding which political figure to support has something to do with character, then we have no candidates. This shouldn't be true. These moral standards have to become essential in America and should be utilized to gain a higher quality of responsibility for this country. This approach heals. It is possible to understand content and character as reputation.

Urban culture is another phrase that identifies Black culture. Urban culture is a slang way of saying African Americans or Blacks are viewed in this way. Urban culture's dialect, music, and fashion are quickly identifiable, and they have been so widely integrated into mainstream pop culture and the broader American culture that it's hard to determine where urban culture ends and the original American culture picks up. At the same time, it seems that more and more middle-class Blacks are explicitly rejecting the accoutrements of Blackness to avoid and dispel the associated stereotypes.

Urban culture has largely morphed into hip-hop culture, which has now become pop culture. There never was a single Black culture. Is urban culture not required to have the same set of evaluation around content of character? Was Martin Luther King only speaking to White America?

There is a Black privilege that we are not held to a higher moral value due to our history of oppression and the history of police brutality. Should a cop be judged by his uniform or the content of his character? Certain stones we only throw in one direction, and in many cases, we have to look in the mirror and apply them to ourselves as a culture. Urban culture should hold the same standard of evaluation, and that is to search a person's character and not give them automatic support because of their race. If we do this, is it not hypocritical to throw this stone of shame toward another race?

There are many different Black cultures. In addition to hip-hop, there is also the culture of the Black middle-class, the Black church, and the Black South. Again, this is not a comprehensive list. The points here are wrapped around the cross-pollination of cultures in America. Consider Tex-Mex, which is some of the best food on the planet. I apologize to the northern states. Tex-Mex is a mix of Mexican food with a Texas progression on it. Once you have your experience, you will desire to move to Texas for this very reason alone. This portion does not help drive my previous points, but I could not proceed without this public service announcement.

I do not believe there is a war on White America, but I would agree there is a war on privilege," and that is possibly and exclusively what is known as "White privilege" What is privilege? White privilege is often presumed to mean that one was financially stable their whole lives and never had to work hard. This is not how it is defined today. It is more of a privilege linked to not have to show empathy toward the challenges or oppressions of other cultures or races—or even consider the impact of certain situations on the lives of others.

The fear minorities feel is not a fear that White America may suffer from in any part of life. It is a privilege to only have to worry about one's own and then to have the luxury that the majority of the outcomes will be favorable. This is privilege. In America, many other cultures have advanced enough so that minorities can experience privilege as well, depending on education level, financial level, where they live, what schools they attend, and many other benefits to their family status growing up.

White privilege is being used as a political narrative now more than a fully weighted threat in our society, and we are suffering from the immunity all other minority groups are receiving for not being held to a certain moral standard. If a White kid walks into his predominately White high school with his pants sagging and says something derogatory toward the teacher, how long will he last before he is in the office and suspended? If a Black kid walks into a high school that is predominately Black and does the same thing, there is a strong possibility he will be reprimanded and sent on to class. In some cases, our own culture's privilege has harmed kids' growth and upbringing more than a White privilege that is not a threat to us at every level of life. So, privilege in any arena can be unfortunate, and it can cause lasting harm. We must address it everywhere, and that includes in all cultural backyards of America.

Privilege: a special right, advantage, or immunity
granted or available only to a person or group.

According to Peggy McIntosh, White privilege refers to the collection of benefits that White people receive in a racially structured society in which they are at the top of the racial hierarchy. Made famous by scholar and activist Peggy McIntosh in 1988, the concept includes everything from whiteness being equated with being familiar and native to the United States to being represented in the media, being trusted, and quickly finding makeup products for one's skin tone. While some might view some of these privileges as trivial, it's essential to recognize that no form of privilege comes without its counterpart: oppression.

Societies can be perceived to be fundamentally structured by race, and understanding one's White privilege or just privilege, regardless of other social characteristics or positions one embodies, is still significant and can grow a person's temperament when even hearing about topics like covering the student loans for all Americans. Given that the meaning of race and the forms that racism takes are ever-evolving in the process of racial formation, it is essential to update our sociological understanding of how White privilege has changed over time.

Are McIntosh's descriptions of White privilege still relevant today? Let review some of her insights:

- The ability to speak and write from an unchallenged position of authority (see, for instance, commenters online).
- The ability to hold onto wealth during the economic crises (Black and Latino families lost far more wealth during the home foreclosure crisis than White families did).

- Protection from experiencing the brunt of negative implications of climate change (economically vulnerable and politically unstable populations, mostly people of color in the global south, are disproportionally affected).
- Protection from the lowest wages and most dangerous labor conditions cultivated by the globalization of production.
- Being able to deny that racism exists.
- Believing in and developing sympathy and empathy for others for "reverse racism."
- Being unconcerned with the racial implications of political candidates one supports.
- Believing you worked hard for and earned everything you have without receiving any help or advantages.
- Believing that people of color who have achieved success have been given racially motivated advantages.
- The ability to adopt a victim status rather than engaging in critical self-reflection when accused of racism.
- Believing it is acceptable to be "ironically" racist.
- Believing that people need to "get over it" or "move on" when they point out racism.
- The belief that cultural products and practices that come from communities of color are yours for the taking.

If we review Prager University's educational pieces around White privilege and some of the speakers employed by Dennis Prager, you will see a totally different argument and perspective on this subject. Since there seems to be a war on "White Privilege" then one of the focus areas is social media. Dennis and many other Conservative Activist are being censored by the platforms for posting things that can be arguably not true, but a perception driven reality for their viewers. Dennis has employed African Americans now to lead many of these conversations, so to not possibly come across as simply a White view, but a conservative view in general. This may also be Dennis's approach in addressing perceptions. One might consider this message a failed attempt if the African American activist sounds exactly like the originator.

If we review McIntosh's description of some examples of "White

Privilege" is to be able to say anything and make that fact because of what race said it. We have seen patterns of this censorship since the election. Is this ok? What I learned with my team at work and how to effectively drive relationship progress was to address the perception. If one feels privileged, they may feel they do not have to do that. Perception review is an effective measure and utility to gain progress in trust with relationships. It is required of every person, if they desire to effectively address the stagnation of the healthy advancement of relationships.

Jesus Christ sat with the Tax Collector to address the perceptions of those he was trying to save. He made sure that a message was sent, that he was no better than they were and sat with them. Even though Jesus Christ was without sin. He sat as a friend with the man full of sin. The conversion in that relationship was remarkably established by this gesture of Love, Sacrifice, and Service. Because the Pharisees hated the tax collectors and sinners, they thought that Jesus should too. The fact that Jesus sat and ate with what was considered the dregs of society was an act of grace that the Pharisees could not comprehend. Jesus did not fear peer pressure from political party affiliates. He cared for the relationship and the soul of even those frowned upon by society.

Matthew 9:9-13 "The Calling of Matthew the Tax Collector" **The Calling of Matthew**

[9] As Jesus went on from there, he saw a man named Matthew sitting at the tax collector's booth. "Follow me," he told him, and Matthew got up and followed him.

[10] While Jesus was having dinner at Matthew's house, many tax collectors and sinners came and ate with him and his disciples. [11] When the Pharisees saw this, they asked his disciples, "Why does your teacher eat with tax collectors and sinners?"

[12] On hearing this, Jesus said, "It is not the healthy who need a doctor, but the sick. [13] But go and learn what this means: 'I desire mercy, not sacrifice.' For I have not come to call the righteous, but sinners."

Dennis and other activist will need to eventually address perceptions. Joe Biden and Kamala Harris will need to address perceptions effectively to bridge the Right and Left. The Healing Process for America will come from taking a step back and addressing perceptions on all sides. These perceptions are someone's reality and they are strong convictions on these perceived realities. I challenged myself years ago to start listening to all views to learn and have more empathy and understanding on all viewpoints.

I have learned a great deal from Prager University, but I would say the speakers for Prager University are not widespread and are more conservative. The strategy is a conservative push and what is genuinely believed to be the best nurture and nature for Americans to thrive in. Does the subject have merit? I believe we must give all views a moment of our time. We can learn and grow. I challenge you to give alternative media from your current views six months of your time. Let your guard down and suppress your pride in this exercise. We do not grow in our comfort zones. We strengthen and grow outside of our comfort zones. The context around White privilege may feel uncomfortable for some. Hang in there. Privilege extends beyond one race and is a characteristic of more fortunate households. This is all done in love. We must move out of comfort zones to grow. Let us examine more.

There are many other ways in which White privilege materializes. Each of us can take a moment to think about the forms of privilege you can see in your life or in the lives of those around you. There very well could be a privilege in many lives of any nationality for those who were raised in wealthier homes and families.

In the political arena today, there is a proposal to pay off student loans. Many Americans believe this is not fair. Many Americans worked hard and saved to pay for their students' college, and they are being penalized if others receive a coverage payment for their debts. While many believe that hard work did enable these options, was privileged involved or an advantage yielded from the previous generation's wealth or good job availability to a particular class of people? Here is one area that privilege could fall into without being noticed and a subliminal battle at large without being defined as a White privilege advantage. The understanding of these areas should help us to pump the brakes and listen to each other to gain peace through this hot topic as it occurs more often in the coming political platforms. I am an African American male. My college tuition was paid for by my parents, and my son's college tuition is being paid for by my parents. Does this make me privileged? If it makes me privileged, does it make me less empathetic and/or racist? It would not offend me to see someone have their student loans forgiven. Everyone does not feel the same way, and that is okay.

Jane Elliott was born on May 27, 1933, and she helps us understand the advantage of White privilege or privilege in general. Jane's experiment targeted one racial class, but it is still relevant for the more fortunate social classes today. I am not justifying a war against privilege here, but I would like to encourage growth and understanding around the subject of privilege so that scientifically one can be set ahead by the environment they were raised in versus the lesser environment another is raised in. This does not mean anyone should apologize for their fortunate upbringing, but maybe one would at least begin to have empathy and agree there are advantages and disadvantages in the environments we grow up in. Her experiment really drives this point home.

Jane Elliot was an American third-grade schoolteacher, anti-racism activist, and educator. She was known for her "blue eye versus brown eyes" exercise. She first conducted her famous exercise for her class on April 5, 1968, the day after Martin Luther King Jr. was assassinated. When her local newspaper published compositions that the children had written about the experience, the reactions (both positive and negative) formed the basis for her career as a public speaker against discrimination.

Elliott's classroom exercise was filmed the third time she held it with her 1970 third-graders to become *The Eye of the Storm*. This inspired a retrospective that reunited the 1970 class members with their teacher fifteen years later in *A Class Divided*. After leaving her school, Elliott became a full-time diversity educator. She still holds the exercise and gives lectures about its effects all over the US and overseas.

On the evening of April 4, 1968, Elliott turned on her television and learned of Dr. Martin Luther King Jr.'s assassination. She says that she vividly remembers a scene in which a White reporter pointed his microphone toward a local Black leader and asked, "When our leader [John F. Kennedy] was killed several years ago, his widow held us together. Who's going to control your people?"

She decided to combine a lesson she had planned about Native Americans with a lesson that she had planned about Dr. Martin Luther

King Jr. for February's Hero of the Month project. As she was watching the news of King's death, Elliott was ironing a teepee for use in a lesson about Native Americans. To tie the two lessons together, she used a Sioux prayer: "Oh great spirit, keep me from ever judging a man until I have walked in his moccasins." She wanted to give her small-town, all-white students the experience of walking in a "colored child's moccasins for a day."

Steven Armstrong was the first child to arrive in Elliott's classroom, and he asked, "Why would they shoot Martin King?" When the rest of the class arrived, Ms. Elliott asked them how they thought it felt to be Black. She suggested to the class that it would be hard for them to understand discrimination without experiencing it themselves, and she asked the children if they would like to find out. The children agreed with a chorus of yeahs. She decided to base the exercise on eye color rather than skin color in order to show the children what racial segregation was like.

On the first day of the exercise, she designated the blue-eyed children as the superior group. Elliott provided brown fabric collars and asked the blue-eyed students to wrap them around the necks of their brown-eyed peers as a method for identifying the minority group easily. She gave the blue-eyed children extra privileges, such as second helpings at lunch, access to the new jungle gym, and five extra minutes at recess. The blue-eyed children sat in the front of the classroom, and the brown-eyed children were sent to sit in the back rows. The blue-eyed children were encouraged to play only with other blue-eyed children and to ignore those with brown eyes. Elliott would not allow brown-eyed and blue-eyed children to drink from the same water fountain and often chastised the brown-eyed students when they did not follow the exercise's rules or made mistakes. She often emphasized the differences between the two groups by singling out students and used negative aspects of brown-eyed children to emphasize a point.

At first, there was resistance among the students in the minority group to the idea that blue-eyed children were better than brown-eyed children. To counter this, Elliott lied to the children by stating that melanin was linked to their higher intelligence and learning ability. Shortly thereafter, this initial resistance fell away. Those who were deemed "superior" became arrogant, bossy, and otherwise unpleasant to their "inferior" classmates. Their grades on simple tests were better, and they completed mathematical and reading tasks that had seemed outside their ability before. The "inferior" classmates also transformed into timid and subservient children who scored more poorly on tests, and even during recess, they isolated themselves, including those who had previously been dominant in the class. These children's academic performance suffered—even with tasks that had been simple before.

The next Monday, Elliott reversed the exercise, making the brown-eyed children superior. While the brown-eyed children did taunt the blue-eyed children in ways like what had occurred the previous day, Elliott reports it was much less intense. At two thirty on Wednesday, Elliott told the blue-eyed children to take off their collars. To reflect on the experience, she asked the children to write down what they had learned. The compositions that the children wrote about the experience were printed in the *Riceville Recorder* on April 18, 1968, under the headline "How Discrimination Feels." The story was picked up by the Associated Press, and Elliott was invited to appear on *The Tonight Show Starring Johnny Carson*. After she spoke about her exercise in a short interview segment, the audience reaction was instant as hundreds of calls came into the show's telephone switchboard, much of it negative. An often-quoted letter stated, "How dare you try this cruel experiment out on White children? Black children grow up accustomed to such behavior, but White children, there's no way they could possibly understand it. It's cruel to White children and will cause them great psychological damage."

Janes message showcased the progress variances between a privileged person vs. an oppressed person. This variance is what is being argued today with systemic racism in America. Some will never fall prey to the challenges of this world, but many will be negatively impacted by it. Such is life? Maybe. Should we have any sympathy or empathy towards what Jane presented in her exercise? On a large scale this exercise is exactly what many are challenging today, and the desire is to even the playing field as much as possible. This can be disruptive and offensive if not carried out with care and remove any shaming of any group of people. Such is life at times. We can do what we can, but no outcome will be perfect.

The publicity that Elliott was getting did not make her popular in Riceville. When she walked into the teachers' lounge the day after her *Tonight Show* appearance, several teachers walked out. When she went downtown to do errands, she heard whispers. When her oldest daughter went to the girls' bathroom in junior high, she came out of a stall to see a hateful message for her scrawled in red lipstick in the mirror.

Of all her coworkers, Elliott states that only one of them, Ruth Setka, continued to speak to her after her exercise went public. Setka said that she realized she was the only one who kept speaking to her. Setka believed that the reason Elliott's exercise got so much backlash was that the students were very young and that the exercise should have been done on at least junior high school-aged students. In a 2003 interview, Elliot said that about 20 percent of the Riceville community was still furious with her over what she did, but she was grateful for the other 80 percent. However, as news of her exercise spread, she appeared on more television shows and started to repeat the exercise in professional training days for adults. On December 15, 1970, Elliott staged the experience to adult educators at a White House Conference on Children and Youth.

In 1970, ABC produced a documentary about Elliott called *The Eye of the Storm*, which made her even more nationally known. William Peters wrote two books—*A Class Divided* and *A Class Divided: Then and Now*—about her and the exercise. *A Class Divided* was turned into a PBS Frontline documentary in 1985 and included a reunion of the schoolchildren featured in *The Eye of the Storm*, for which Elliott received The Hillman Prize.

A televised edition of the exercise was shown in the United Kingdom on October 29, 2009, on Channel 4 entitled "The Event: How Racist Are You?" This documentary was intended, according to the producers in their agreement with Jane Elliott, to create an awareness of the effects of racist behaviors by using British citizens. After the exercise, Elliott said that the result "wasn't as successful as I am accustomed to being," leaving journalist Andrew Anthony with the "nagging suspicion that she's more excited by White fear than she is by black success." Elliott was featured by Peter Jennings on ABC as "Person of the Week" on April 24, 1992. She is listed on the timeline of thirty notable educators by textbook editor McGraw-Hill along with Confucius, Plato, Booker T. Washington, and Maria Montessori. She has been invited to speak at 350 colleges and universities and has appeared on *The Oprah Winfrey Show* five times. In November 2016, Elliott's name was added to the BBC's annual list of 100 Women.

Jane Elliot's experiment allows us to see the impact on one group of people, just based on how they are treated, having a long-term effect on character.

In America today this should yield empathy to understanding what many African Americans or still struggling with. Long-term effects of being marginalized by society. Liberals at times seem to get this, but often Conservatives seem to drive a perception, that it should no longer be an issue. African Americans can be limited in how they are defined by a certain political class. If Liberals launch campaigns that African American communities need help, then the message might say relief is coming, but it also might say "do nothing until I am elected to help you". Conservatives will say, I am going to remove government restraints and give you an opportunity to fend for yourselves and prosper. If you are victorious, great. If you fail that will be on you. These are all perspectives to think about and I am not stating them as absolute facts. Let us grow.

Sanjay Gupta recently had a documentary called "Stress in America," and one of the experiments composed in the documentary was with two monkeys. The monkeys were given a rock in two separate cages, and when prompted, they were to give the rock back to their keeper to get a cucumber. The next day, they were given the same rock, and when prompted, they were to give it to the keeper and get a red grape. The third day, one of the monkeys was given the cucumber for giving the rock back, and the other monkey was given a red grape for giving the rock back. The monkey that received the cucumbers for giving the rock back started to get very upset as he saw the other monkey was receiving grapes. He eventually threw the cucumber back at the keeper and started hitting and rattling the cage in anger. This unfairness aroused the monkey's anger. In the conclusion of this experiment, we learned that it is natural for one to feel anger or frustration from being maltreated to the point of rage. Does this explain riots? It probably will not explain looting, but it could gain some ground on empathy with riots.

American culture was built initially on "law and order." It has been said that riots are the language of the unheard. Many will say that the rioters were not wanting to be heard, but they were seeking to loot and exercise violence at a time when it might be given a leverage of justification. Has America failed to hear the silent, peaceful protests of the NFL? Has America failed to hear the peaceful protests of the Black Lives Matter movement? Did we turn a deaf ear to these protests because they violated the approach we would have desired for us to listen?

Would Jesus have listened to the cry of these movements? Are these individuals our neighbors? Are they deserving of a moment of empathy from Americans? Would a listening ear have helped reduce if not eliminate these protest, riots, and movements? Have you ever experienced a troubled teen in your household finally getting so frustrated with their parents that they destroy something in their room or in the home?

Counselors see that an overwhelmingly majority of America's troubled teens will say they feel they do not have a voice and no one in their home listens to them. As a father, I experienced this with my own son. My son did not destroy anything, but he did get infuriated with me once and explained that it was because I never let him speak his side. I began to allow my son to have his say, and I sincerely took into consideration his side of the story. I noticed how his body language became vulnerable, and I even saw tears a few times. I realized my pattern of being the hard dad and treating my son the way I was treated as a child. I was raised to be tough, and I didn't have a voice or a say-so.

Many African American males have grown up in households that did not allow them to have feelings or voices. When they got out of the house, they were going to treat their own kids the same way or lose their tempers during frustrating moments.

Have you ever heard about the so-called angry Black man? It is not in our DNA; it is from a pattern of being treated harshly even in our own households. A mother and father or even a fatherless household where it was tough and the frustration from Mom trying to hold everything together seems to be relived on the children of those households. They grow up with constant frustration, and they begin to see the peacefulness of Whites and believe in White privilege. They see this as unfair and can become envious of that cultural upbringing or bitter about it.

A police officer could teach him temperance or confront him. This is a recipe for confrontation. No one really wants the confrontation, but there are so many variables on the table that it becomes the perfect storm for something unfortunate.

My dad was hard on me as kid. He wanted to help me be strong one day and to be able to deal with adversity. My dad also wanted to place fear in me to give me self-preservation in times of dealing with authority. That is not every African American kid's upbringing in America. What if a police officer does not understand this dynamic of an African American male's life? What if he does not accept it as an excuse or opportunity for empathy?

America, have we failed to listen to the movement's issue about police brutality, injustice, and oppression—whether we agree with it or not? In many cases, I did not agree with my son's version of the story. He is my son, and I love him—so I listened anyway. Once I listened to him, I gained his trust—and now I can be his dad and offer advice. When I didn't listen to my son, it was not going to be as effective in giving him advice and he was less likely to take into consideration what I had to say.

Today, I listen to him every time we have a challenging situation, and we progress through those challenges in a very healthy way. It feels like love in its highest form. Listening can do that? Yes! Listening is the absolute guarantee of riot prevention. If we consider Dr. King's words as evidence and truth, then we would have to take responsibility for the riots when they happen if we postponed or prolonged justice.

I do not believe America would have reacted in such a way if the killer (police officer) of George Floyd had been taken into custody the same day. This may be an option moving forward in all killings of unarmed men in America. The police officer or individual may be taken into custody immediately until a four- or five-day investigation is conducted. That is just a thought.

Chicago has one of the highest homicides rates in America. Illinois also has a the some of the strictest gun laws. Chicago is historically Democrat. If you examine crime in America, it is significantly higher in Democratic-led metroplexes. Why is that? Conservative posture is one of law and order as a high priority. In today's climate, this thought is somewhat offensive.

Conservative posture is also one of pro-gun and the right to protect yourself. Imagine the Chicago gang violence in Texas? Texas is a pro-gun state. Considering where the homicides would take place, the pro-gun outfit of Texas would combat some of the violence on its own—if not significantly deter it. One might think twice before starting to shoot to kill in Texas on a regular basis. This doesn't mean Texas doesn't have its share of homicides, but the culture here says that one must be aware that everyone can have a gun and has a culture of no fear in using them to protect and defend.

When it comes to mass shootings, Texas had its own at Santa Fe High School. In essence, we are not fully protected from the unpredictability of one disturbed person. I share all of this so that we might see that just because one group is against guns and drives the fear factor, it doesn't automatically equate to safer. Chicago is not safe in some areas, and there are fewer guns. The bad guys have the guns.

Jeffery Shaun King, an American writer, civil rights activist, and cofounder of Real Justice PAC, made a profound statement after the protests over the George Floyd killing:

> Stop generically telling us to "vote" in response to all of the police brutality we have right now. Yes, we should vote, but we have to be very specific. Democrats, from top to bottom, are running the cities with the worst of the police brutality in America right now. We voted for them.
>
> We must vote for the people that love us, and will stand for the policies, no matter what, that will protect us, and help us thrive. That's not what we have right now, period. We have to get way more specific on who and what we are voting for.

I am not choosing a political side here. I am showing the case of someone who is no longer leaning toward the perception or the fear factors that we traditionally are reacting to. Shaun is saying we need to understand better. Without saying too much, I would say he is saying African Americans need to research and make an educated decision about their votes and not just give it to Democrats if it is not serving them well statistically.

I am sure Shaun King would dispute what I just said. Perception and fear factors lead most of the African American communities to automatically support Democrats. In November 2018, Shaun King stated that he was 99 percent sure he would not support Joe Biden and Kamala Harris as candidates for president due to their history of advancing incarceration of African Americans during their times of service.

In 2020 Shaun King said he is honored to support a brilliant Black woman as the vice presidential nominee. I would say that 99 percent saves Shaun from falling back on any promise, but it also drives perception of what shifted his support. Was it race? Maybe it was just the thought that he cannot for any reason support a republican or Donald Trump.

We are in times when many people support and vote in their comfort zones and support their propaganda they are pushing. "Blexit" (Black exit) is a movement that encourages African American voters to leave the Democratic Party and/or at least the loyalty to voting Democrat and become more educated on the historical data to what has actually been credited to each party over the years.

Founders Candace Owens and Brandon Tatum came together because of their shared desire to build a better future for America, Americans, and African Americans. Candace and Brandon are often demonized and not given a platform to speak to African Americans without contention or discourse due to the perception of their tones of outside-the-box thinking and nonurban-conforming systems of expression.

I would say Shaun King has experienced his own demonization as well from the right. They both seek to educate minorities across America about the history of our great country by highlighting the principles of the Constitution of the United States and the importance of self-reliance. What is the new "woke" that many in urban culture speak of? Can the new woke be a deeper investigation in the history of the two parties? Could African Americans be living a life of manipulation at this point in the upcoming election so that their votes stay locked in, uninformed?

If one is to heal properly, I would say with all due respect, we cannot have automatic voting towards our comfort zones. Healing allows us to hear all arguments and allows our votes to be earned by sound statistics and not by manipulated perceptions and feelings.

Stop making a culture of law enforcement with full immunity a challengeable item. No law enforcement agent should be given full immunity, but we also have to be careful not to offend the culture of it and communicate respectfully how to protect the public against clear acts of abuse of force, perception removed.

One in a thousand Black men and boys in America can expect to die at the hands of police, according to a new analysis of deaths involving law enforcement officers since a study in 2019 by the *Los Angeles Times*. Statistically, that makes Black men and boys 2.5 times more likely than White men and boys to die during an encounter with law enforcement officers. The point is that everything is not perception. We have to consider that we do not fully know the details of each of these cases, but the number is significant.

We must always consider if the decision we are making is freedom of speech or protest or staging war on a particular culture. If it is, we have to consider a more gentle and milder approach. Share the knowledge of that culture and figure out why there is a respectful need to shift. This approach will allow it to be better received, and one might gain agreement.

Show respect and honor first—and then give your reasoning. With each passionate notion stemming from each controversial event in America, we have to be sure our measurements, remedies, and reconciliations steer clear of culture items as much as possible. Cultural challenges will rarely end in positive feelings.

Guns are a culture in America. Supporting police officers is a culture. The American flag, the Pledge of Allegiance, and the National Anthem are all cultures in America. We must consider the harm and damages that will come with challenging certain cultural statutes in America. Does this mean no cultural areas can be challenged? It does not. Seeing a Confederate flag causes some people to be offended or even threatened. Maybe this is one that can be challenged, but it is still culture, and we must be prepared for the ght and approach these topics with care. We are here to grow and heal. The approach is everything.

What does God have to say: Was there a war on cultures and racism in the Bible?

In *A Time to Kill*, the character played by Matthew McConaughey faced a challenge. To win a case, he had to convince the jury of their own prejudices and then ask them to imagine the girl being raped as a "White girl." Once the jury closed their eyes and imagined the little girl being raped as a "White girl," they suddenly had compassion and saw the value in the human being.

Regarding "unarmed" Black men being shot or killed by police officers, these are the same cases. The dividing line is peer pressure, comfort zones, and traditional cultural prejudices. Society will not have concerns or compassion until they change the image of the person affected into something (pet, animal) or someone they value.

Even Christians struggle with separating traditional political and cultural comfort zones to do what is right and avoid their prejudices. The disciple Peter had the same struggle, and he walked with Christ:

> When Peter came to Antioch, I told him face to face that he was wrong. He used to eat with Gentile followers of the Lord until James sent some Jewish followers. Peter was afraid of the Jews and soon stopped eating with Gentiles. He and the other Jews hid their true feelings so well that even Barnabas was fooled. But when I saw that they were not really obeying the truth that is in the good news, I corrected Peter in front of everyone and said: "Peter, you are a Jew, but you live like a Gentile. So how can you force Gentiles to live like Jews?" (Galatians 2:11–14 NIV)

Peter felt the pressure to go back to living in the standard Jewish political traditions and customs and drop the Gospel and the Gentiles for fear of the Jews frowning upon him. This still happens in modern churches with Christians from different upbringings. It divides the body of Christ (the church) and renders the Gospel powerless to convert and encourage. Unity in Christ was speaking of these divisions (Ephesians 4).

When we take allegiance with a political party or human traditions, we put down the Gospel. We do what Peter did. Peter wanted to continue to be accepted by those he grew up with. Peter turned his back on his own brothers in Christ to go back into his comfort zone. Today, many Christian brothers and sisters have taken that same position to be accepted by their social network of friends and family.

To move forward and heal as a nation, our comfort zones must diminish and nonpartisan postures must rise. People must regard others in higher esteem and swallow and dissolve their egos and pride.

FIVE

No Understanding, No Peace

No Christ, No Peace. Know Christ, Know Peace. Today we have the ability, to fact check everything, but instead we do not if the translator of the message says what we already agree with or believe. We trust in whom we are comfortable with in delivering information. The media that speaks to our culture, our comfort zones, and the ones who are sensitive to our way of life, becomes the trusted communication of national news updates. There are threats of exiting any news cast that does not say what we would rather hear. Entitlement Generation is here. We are entitled to be pleased every day. No disappointments allowed today. No character desired. Could this be from a generation that was spoiled by parents and grandparents? Is this safe or does it bind us to one way of thinking? One way of thinking cannot be healthy and or sustainable. If we have committed to one way of thinking, then can we ever grow? Is this an automatic formula for dis-trust. It has become just that. If I cannot relate to Fox news, I feel offended by Fox news, and Fox news seems to be off task with the challenges I have, then I cannot trust them. We then yield power to Fox news. This also goes for those who do not wish to watch CNN. *I get it. Both sides, I get it. "Biased News"* has plagued America. The strategy is to drive "fear" that your comfort zone and way of life is at risk or in jeopardy of being taken away from you. "What are you going to do about it", The Fire Starter says. Then the Flame Fanners re-post and re-post. Here we go. Only the first responders can save the day, by not responding. We are being driven by biasness. We are not being driven by emotional intelligent responses and reactions.

Here is a big question. *Why?* We are on the cutting edge of technology to be able to research any and everything. Why would we not utilize our options to look deeper into each "hot" event in America to understand it better? Have we gotten lazy and fall to our comfort zones of media diets? It is time to grow. Growth requires us to step outside of our comfort zones and listen to others. Listen to the other side sometimes. Research. Look things up with an open mind. When we try and understand our neighbor, we can now have peace with our neighbor. Let us consider Jammer again in chapter one. What was taking away his peace? Was it the low amount of his raise or was it just him not understanding the reason behind the low amount of his raise? We restore our personal power through understanding, and we stay mentally exhausted through constant disputing of personal battles of vindication or justification. If "we" try and understand others, "we" will begin to heal. America, let us listen to understand each other and not listen to respond.

Proverbs 11:12 (NIV) states that whoever derides their neighbor has no sense, but the one who has understanding holds their tongue. If you understand something or a situation, you might not speak as quickly about the situation. Whoever provokes their neighbor has no sense.

God teaches us to love our neighbors, and this is not the person next door, but the stranger you do not know. In the parable of the Good Samaritan, the man beaten and left for dead was a stranger and not the neighbor next door.

Most of us only know the world we were born into, which means the culture that surrounded us from childhood. We must challenge ourselves to understand more. Understanding will be the solution that brings peace. We must begin to investigate and part ways from identifying ourselves immediately with our comfort zones and the cultures that are a part of that comfort zone.

There is a whole other reality out there for most Americans. That reality can be the polar opposite of yours. This doesn't make it bad or more challenging, but it is different. When we try to understand another person's reality, we find an opportunity for empathy. Simply sitting down for a cup of coffee or lunch with someone of opposing views will accomplish a lot. Get to know each other. Empathy or a trusting relationship might allow for a person to say, "Black lives matter," without us feeling threatened by those words. Empathy and understanding might allow for a person to not be shamed for their political stances.

America is great because of its diversity and inclusion, but it was built by something totally different. If we wanted to repair a car or a lawnmower or any other household item, we have now become the YouTube maintenance generation. We go to YouTube or Google to understand how to fix things. The healing of America will take some research and investigation into the issues to rely on factual information instead of political ideologies. This can no longer be about who's right; it has to begin to be about what is right. What is right is that we find common ground and begin to love each other in spite of our differences. Agape is a sacrificial love that Jesus Christ had for the world. In spite of how you feel about him, he died for us all. It will not be difficult to find common ground. We mostly all want the same things in life, much of which is fair opportunity, safety, education, food, and shelter.

Fact-checking is the act of checking factual assertions in a nonfictional text in order to determine the veracity and correctness of the factual statements in the text. If we are to go deeper into understanding to gain peace, maybe we need to do our own fact-checking on a more detailed scale. There are options for going further in depth to find out truths and false statements. This may be done either before or after the text has been published or otherwise disseminated. Fact-checking before dissemination aims to remove errors and allow a text to proceed to dissemination or to rejection if it fails confirmations or other criteria. Post hoc fact-checking is often followed by a written report of inaccuracies—sometimes with a visual metric from the checking organization.

External post hoc fact-checking by independent organizations began in the United States in the early 2000s. In the 2010s, particularly following the 2016 election of Donald Trump as president, fact-checking gained a rise in popularity and spread to multiple countries in Europe and Latin America. However, the United States remains the largest market for fact-checking. One study finds that fact-checkers PolitiFact, FactCheck.org, and the *Washington Post*'s Fact Checker are frequently visited platforms that help citizens be more informed.

Research on the impact of fact-checking is relatively recent, but the existing research suggests that fact-checking does correct misperceptions among citizens and discourages politicians from spreading misinformation. Fact-checking is a political tool that has been used throughout history, and it should be used. There has even been a pop culture phenomenon of "truth-o-meters."

One study has shown that fact-checking has been diluted and tarnished by a "politi-fact approach," which means an investigation with a biased eye for the truth. The fact-checking phenomenon has gone global. In Africa, there is Africa Check, Africa's first independent fact-checking organization with offices in Kenya, Nigeria, South Africa, Senegal, and the UK to check claims made by public figures and the media in Africa. In India, there is Boom, which is a fact-checking digital journalism website. GoHoo is a fact-checking group launched by a nonprofit association, Watchdog for Accuracy in News-Reporting, in Japan. Iran has Gomaneh, an online Persian magazine devoted to the investigation of rumors and hearsay. Latin America has Argentina's Chequeado.com, and Central America has Rete al candidato. In the US, we even have PolitiFact to rate the accuracy or claims of all statements made by politicians. Let us consider this during this craze.

In terms of the topics that are hot right now, I like a statement made by Randall Stephenson, the CEO of AT&T. He stated we should try to "listen" and not respond with a counterstatement like "All lives matter" and try to understand the pain behind the Black Lives Matter movement. With an investigation to fact-find more on the hot topics of this nation, we may find peace and resolve problems. We are all potential fools when we act, respond, and communicate without doing any research. It has been said that 60 percent of our thoughts are self-directed; 30 percent of our thoughts are wrapped around relationships we have with family, friends, and associates; and 10 percent is related to empathy. These percentages are considering the divisions of thought. Here are some considerations to have when dealing with people.

- Never blame malicious intent for what can easily be explained by conceit.
- Few social behaviors are explicit.
- Behaviors are largely dictated by selfish altruism.
- People have poor memories.
- Everyone is emotional.
- People are lonely.
- People are self-absorbed.

Most of these considerations are more about people focused on themselves and not about ourselves, but we are so absorbed in ourselves that we think everything is about us. It is a vicious cycle of conflict. During your next conflict, stop for a second and tell yourself that what you feel is more about you than them, and what they said is more about them than you! Conflict solved? Maybe.

If you make an effort to understand, there will be a greater opportunity for peace. If you do not make a reasonable effort to try to understand, there will be the potential for a disturbance, tension, or anguish with no peace. When people are in anguish, they do not understand the in-depth meaning of something they are experiencing. Today, we simply proceed forward and accuse others of what is really our own confusion around their stance or posture toward a hot topic. Due to this confusion, you are in anguish. Nobody is in anguish because of others; it is because of their own discernment of a situation. We feel anguish because we do not understand, which yields no peace.

My father and I used to have many moments of contention once I became an adult. We got along better when I was a child and a teenager. In my twenties, he and I could not get along for any extended period of time. I tried to analyze it spiritually and to think deeper about the causes, but I could not find a reason to allow him to dominate me as an adult.

When we would decide to go to a family reunion or to eat breakfast after church, the decision was dominated by my father. We would end up quarrelling about the venue or the time we would leave or what we were taking.

Later in life, my father-in-law told me to be more flexible with my parents and my father. "Show him some grace," he said. "If you do that, he will become more understanding or at least you will."

I was confused. *If I allow him to control and dominate me, how will he learn that this is unacceptable?* I was trying to fix my dad and teach him a lesson. We were both trying to dominate these situations, and I was losing. *How can me being more flexible help?*

We both wanted the final say or the ultimate decision. As an adult now, I believed I should be allowed to sometimes decide where we eat or what time we were going to leave.

You could waste your life if you try to change others. They will suffer if they are not understanding, but why should you suffer the same fate? Both people end up suffering due to not wanting to tap out to the other. We call these relationships toxic, and the essence of toxicity is your view an attitude about a situation. Everybody is trying to dominate. If you drop out of it, your struggle will disappear.

In today's political climate, each side is trying to dominate. Neither side will allow for any grace toward the other side. We should begin to learn that a person's behavior has more to do with their internal struggles than it has to do with us. If we learn this, we will begin to exemplify grace. God yields this same grace to us as Christians in the hope that we will yield it to someone else.

Grace can become contagious if we showcase it. The toxicity of stubbornness to dominate each other destroys the peace in America—just as it did with my relationship with my father. Who will win? In the end, there will be no winner. There will only be scars and pain. Grace wins, and love wins—and it gives us hope for a higher quality of life. Before you give an uninformed response, give grace. Give silence and a listening ear. This is love. Watch the outcome. You could gain a friend instead of an enemy.

If we try to understand each other, we can escape domination, aggression, violence, and anger. It is easy to judge. It is more difficult to try to understand. Understanding requires compassion, patience, and a sincere willingness to believe that good hearts are still allowed to have different opinions, different methods, and different outlooks. When we judge, we separate—and growth is suppressed. When we gain understanding, we begin to grow. It is easier not to be wise.

Giving grace and flexibility to those with opposing views or dominating approaches is difficult, but a positive, silent distance will allow peace without real change. When there is change, you can look at things and laugh. You will feel relief that you now have the power over what was causing you so much anguish. You let it go. You get out the ring. You take off your boxing gloves and strategize. How ridiculous have we been? Laugh. It's okay.

We often think the whole world is wrong and/or the opposing view is wrong. *If I could change their thought, the world would be a better place for them and me—and then I would be happy.* This is a shallow and ignorant point of view, respectfully. This will result in a life of consistent unhappiness. Once you understand that the battle is not for your higher quality of life—and it has removed a significant portion of your higher quality of life—you will find value in changing yourself and letting others be. To simply change the whole world, the only thing you can do is change yourself and achieve what you desire. Sadly enough, vindication is the real root and driver of anguish. Show grace and flexibility, as my father-in-law said, and you will find peace each time you enact this powerful move.

How do we begin to understand each other? The most loving people you will encounter in your lifetime have known defeat, suffering, struggle, and loss, but they have found their way out of the depths. These experiences cause a maturation to take place in a person's life. This individual will begin to have an appreciation, a sensitivity, and an understanding of life that fills them with compassion, gentleness, and a deep, loving concern.

Understanding will come with listening. We hear each other today, but we rarely listen. Listening is giving one's attention to sound; examples include speech, music, or natural sounds. Listening involves complex affective, cognitive, and behavioral processes. Effective processes include the motivation to attend to others; cognitive processes include attending to, understanding, receiving, and interpreting content and relational messages; and behavioral processes include responding with verbal and nonverbal feedback.

Effective listening may even require unbiased research or an investigation into some of the statements you have heard. Peace is a daily, weekly, and monthly process with gradually changing opinions that slowly erode old barriers and eventually become new evolved beliefs. We must understand that peace cannot be retained by force. The beauty about peace is that it can be willingly achieved through understanding.

Darkness cannot drive out darkness; only light can do that. Hate cannot drive out hate; only love can do that. That yields numberless acts of courage and an evolved belief that human history is reshaped each time a person stands up for an ideal view and then acts upon that view to improve the experiences others will be subjected to. This may require a strike against injustice that may offend cultures as it sends forth a major ripple of hope, contending with a million different centers of energy that oppose this view. These ripples build a current that can sweep down the mightiest walls of oppression and resistance toward healthy change. It's ugly, and it's uncomfortable—but it is essential for change.

The birthrights to peace can come from being able to contribute the best we have—and all that we are—toward creating a world that supports everyone. In addition to these efforts, it is securing the space for others to contribute the best they have and all that they are if it is open to diversity and inclusion. If you want to make peace with your enemy, you have to learn to work with your enemy. If you do, you become partners and can enhance the experience of the atmosphere around you both. There is peace in understanding. With understanding, we must establish a social contract with each other. In the face of conflict, we balance powers by considering each side's interests, listening, and allowing this cooperation to align with our expectations that all conflicts can be resolved. This does not mean anyone won or lost, but if you keep a friend, we win. If we lose a friend, no one wins.

Martin Luther King accepted his Nobel Peace Prize with a speech of full understanding and optimism wrapped around his experience in the civil rights movement in America. He was not at all regretful of the harsh things he experienced; he was grateful for the option to protest, rally, speak, and organize. Martin deserved the Nobel Peace Prize for being an activist and evangelist for equal rights and peaceful protest and for the very nature of his attitude and patience towards change. His inner peace was a jewel that needed to be recognized. His inner peace was powerful. He understood the challenges he faced. I encourage readers to find Dr. King's Nobel Peace Prize acceptance speech online, watch it, and return to this book.

Understanding is the key to peace—or at least it should be. If we can consider these words of MLK, one would grow immediately in a posture toward a solution for injustice toward fellow Americans. Dr King understood all the oppression he faced, yet he remained optimistic as he moved forward. Understanding doesn't mean we agree; it means we know enough to respect each other's positions or at least respect to be different.

Let us examine one more area of understanding. There is a perception that minorities mostly vote Democrat. One would say 100 percent sure that Martin Luther King would have voted Democrat. Why is this? Is it because minorities align with Democrats—or are there external events that drive these selections of candidates?

Political parties are always looking for endorsements from community leaders and other influencers. Having support from prominent figures can make or break a candidate or a party. It's no surprise that political groups sometimes try to claim affiliations with historical figures. Which party did Martin Luther King Jr. support? The official answer is neither. King talked very infrequently about his personal politics and was not formally affiliated with either political party. He did not explicitly endorse any candidate. In fact, he stated, "I don't think the Republican Party is a party full of the almighty God, nor is the Democratic Party. They both have weaknesses. And I'm not inextricably bound to either party."

The political parties of King's time were different from the parties we know today; policies and platforms have changed drastically over time. According to King biographer David J. Garrow, King was fond of some Republican politicians, such as Richard Nixon, although it is almost certain that King voted for Democrats John F. Kennedy in 1960 and Lyndon Johnson in 1964.

Among the few times he ventured into open partisanship was to denounce Republican presidential candidate Barry Goldwater, who, as a senator, had voted against the Civil Rights Act of 1964. King said, "I had no alternative but to urge every Negro and White person of goodwill to vote against Mr. Goldwater and to withdraw support from any Republican candidate that did not publicly disassociate himself from Senator Goldwater and his philosophy."

Although King supported Johnson's presidential campaign, he later spoke out about his dissatisfaction with Johnson's handling of the Vietnam War. That King was often tight-lipped about his personal politics does not mean that he was not passionate about politics. His commitment to social and economic justice for African Americans defined his career, and he frequently expressed skepticism toward capitalism. He said, "A nation that continues year after year to spend more money on military defense than on programs of social uplift is approaching spiritual death."

King was intensely invested in increasing African Americans voters, heading a group in the late 1950s that aimed to register new African American voters in the South. So, if you want to closely align your political practice with that of King, perhaps the best way would be registering to vote and ensuring that others have the right to do the same.

Year over year, my values align with Republican/conservative candidates, even though I do not always support the republican candidate nominee. Imagine that. I am voting against my own values. I have voted in a fashion of how I feel about the candidate's posture towards my race or financial demographics. I do not agree with abortion. I believe prayer should be in schools. I believe in traditional marriages, but I also believe in the right for everyone to have the same benefits and respect as any other person. I agree we should have a border wall. I believe in stricter laws on immigration. I believe in global warming. I believe women should be paid a fair wage that is comparable to men's salaries. I will respect whatever the law provides and protects. Like Dr. King, I do not identify as a Republican or a Democrat. I would prefer to be identified as a Christian, an imperfect man, and a servant. My vote is cast on feelings more than sound moral values. I believe many decide this way.

Identify your negative qualities that do not allow America to be great or you to be great. What are you ashamed of? This takes courage to share, and it also takes humility. Share on social media and ask for forgiveness. Make it public. Post the steps you will take to work on those areas of your life to become a better citizen, teammate, friend, family member, employee, church member, or neighbor. Being humble is one of the most important characteristics one can have. We must show it.

Let's put this chapter subject matter to the test. Today many of us may feel under attack. We have resolved this to be stress from the Left and the Right depending on your political appetite, and arguably a hot climate being fanned or lit by our Commander and Chief. There is some credibility in this, but is there any good at all from the current presidency? Let's examine. Donald Trump took office in 2016. As the president of the United States and so has he done anything good!

In 2008 the Dow Jones was at 11,957.00 and it grew to 17,927.11 by

2016. This was under Obama. From 2016 the Dow Jones has grown as high as 30,000.00 plus pre-pandemic under Trump. Both Presidents have done a great job at advancing the economy. Trump exceedingly has grown it the most over 4 years in comparison to Obama over 8 years. We can only hope that the next 4 years, we stay on the same progression. If America is to heal, we should live in such a way that we do not avoid or fear giving any opposing party credit where credit is due or have a spirit to encourage areas that have benefited Americans and this is regardless of political views. We struggle with giving the opposing party any credit. This is not good. Let's examine accomplishments of what might be for some an opposing party's results.

1. Trump's EPA gave $100 million to fix the water infrastructure problem in Flint, Michigan.
2. Under Trump's leadership, in 2018 the U.S. surpassed Russia and Saudi Arabia to become the world's largest producer of crude oil.
3. Trump signed a law ending the gag orders on pharmacists that prevented them from sharing money-saving information.
4. Trump signed a bill to require airports to provide spaces for breastfeeding moms.
5. The 25% lowest-paid Americans enjoyed a 4.5% income boost in November 2019, which outpaces a 2.9% gain in earnings for the country's highest-paid workers.
6. Low-wage workers are benefiting from higher minimum wages and from corporations that are increasing entry-level pay.
7. Trump signed the biggest wilderness protection & conservation bill in a decade and designated 375,000 acres as protected land.
8. Trump signed the Save our Seas Act which funds $10 million per year to clean tons of plastic & garbage from the ocean.
9. He signed a bill this year allowing some drug imports from Canada so that prescription prices would go down.
10. Trump signed an executive order this year that forces all healthcare providers to disclose the cost of their services so that Americans can comparison shop and know how much less providers charge insurance companies.

11. When signing that bill, he said no American should be blindsided by bills for medical services they never agreed to in advance.

12. Hospitals will now be required to post their standard charges for services, which include the discounted price a hospital is willing to accept.

13. In the eight years prior to President Trump's inauguration, prescription drug prices increased by an average of 3.6% per year. Under Trump, drug prices have seen year-over-year declines in nine of the last ten months, with a 1.1% drop as of the most recent month.

14. He created a White House VA Hotline to help veterans and principally staffed it with veterans and direct family members of veterans.

15. VA employees are being held accountable for poor performance, with more than 4,000 VA employees removed, demoted, and suspended so far.

16. Issued an executive order requiring the Secretaries of Defense, Homeland Security, and Veterans Affairs to submit a joint plan to provide veterans access to access to mental health treatment as they transition to civilian life.

17. Trump recently signed three bills to benefit Native people. One gives compensation to the Spokane tribe for loss of their lands in the mid-1900s, one funds Native language programs, and the third gives federal recognition to the Little Shell Tribe of Chippewa Indians in Montana.

18. Trump finalized the creation of Space Force as our 6th Military branch.

19. Trump signed a law to make cruelty to animals a federal felony so that animal abusers face tougher consequences.

20. Violent crime has fallen every year he's been in office after rising during the two years before he was elected.

21. Because of a bill signed and championed by Trump, in 2020, most federal employees will see their pay increase by an average of 3.1% — the largest raise in more than 10 years.

22. Trump signed into a law up to 12 weeks of paid parental leave for millions of federal workers.

23. Trump administration will provide HIV prevention drugs for free to 200,000 uninsured patients per year for 11 years.

24. Record sales during the 2019 holidays.

25. Trump signed an order allowing small businesses to group together when buying insurance to get a better price.

26. President Trump signed the Preventing Maternal Deaths Act that provides funding for states to develop maternal mortality reviews to better understand maternal complications and identify solutions & largely focuses on reducing the higher mortality rates for Black Americans.

27. In 2018, President Trump signed the groundbreaking First Step Act, a criminal justice bill which enacted reforms that make our justice system fairer and help former inmates successfully return to society.

28. The First Step Act's reforms addressed inequities in sentencing laws that disproportionately harmed Black Americans and reformed mandatory minimums that created unfair outcomes.

29. The First Step Act expanded judicial discretion in sentencing of non-violent crimes.

30. Over 90% of those benefiting from the retroactive sentencing reductions in the First Step Act are Black Americans.

31. The First Step Act provides rehabilitative programs to inmates, helping them successfully rejoin society and not return to crime.

32. Trump increased funding for historically Black Colleges and Universities (HBCUs) by more than 14%.

33. Trump signed legislation forgiving Hurricane Katrina debt that threatened HBCUs.

34. New single-family home sales are up 31.6% in October 2019 compared to just one year ago.

35. Made HBCUs a priority by creating the position of executive director of the White House Initiative on HBCUs.

36. Trump received the Bipartisan Justice Award at a historically black college for his criminal justice reform accomplishments.

37. The poverty rate fell to a 17-year low of 11.8% under the Trump administration as a result of a jobs-rich environment.

38. Poverty rates for African Americans and Hispanic-Americans have reached their lowest levels since the U.S. began collecting such data.

39. President Trump signed a bill that creates five national monuments, expands several national parks, adds 1.3 million acres of wilderness, and permanently reauthorizes the Land and Water Conservation Fund.

40. Trump's USDA committed $124 Million to rebuild rural water infrastructure.

41. [Prior to the unexpected coronavirus pandemic] Consumer confidence & small business confidence is at an all-time high.

42. [Prior to the unexpected coronavirus pandemic] More than 7 million jobs created since election.

43. [Prior to the unexpected coronavirus pandemic] More Americans were employed than ever recorded before in our history.

44. More than 400,000 manufacturing jobs created since his election.

45. Trump appointed five openly gay ambassadors.

46. Trump ordered Ric Grenfell, his openly gay ambassador to Germany, to lead a global initiative to decriminalize homosexuality across the globe.

47. Through Trump's Anti-Trafficking Coordination Team (ACTeam) initiative, Federal law enforcement more than doubled convictions of human traffickers and increased the number of defendants charged by 75% in ACTeam districts.

48. In 2018, the Department of Justice (DOJ) dismantled an organization that was the internet's leading source of prostitution-related advertisements resulting in sex trafficking.

49. Trump's OMB published new anti-trafficking guidance for government procurement officials to more effectively combat human trafficking.

50. Trump's Immigration and Customs Enforcement's Homeland Security Investigations arrested 1,588 criminals associated with Human Trafficking.

51. Trump's Department of Health and Human Services provided funding to support the National Human Trafficking Hotline to identify perpetrators and give victims the help they need.

52. The hotline identified 16,862 potential human trafficking cases.

53. Trump's DOJ provided grants to organizations that support human trafficking victims – serving nearly 9,000 cases from July 1, 2017, to June 30, 2018.

54. The Department of Homeland Security has hired more victim assistance specialists, helping victims get resources and support.

55. President Trump has called on Congress to pass school choice legislation so that no child is trapped in a failing school because of his or her zip code.

56. The President signed funding legislation in September 2018 that increased funding for school choice by $42 million.

57. The tax cuts signed into law by President Trump promote school choice by allowing families to use 529 college savings plans for elementary and secondary education.

58. Under his leadership ISIS has lost most of their territory and been largely dismantled.

59. ISIS leader Abu Bakr Al-Baghdadi was killed.

60. Signed the first Perkins CTE reauthorization since 2006, authorizing more than $1 billion for states each year to fund vocational and career education programs.

61. Executive order expanding apprenticeship opportunities for students and workers.

62. Trump issued an Executive Order prohibiting the U.S. government from discriminating against Christians or punishing expressions of faith.

63. Signed an executive order that allows the government to withhold money from college campuses deemed to be anti-Semitic and who fail to combat anti-Semitism.

64. President Trump ordered a halt to U.S. tax money going to international organizations that fund or perform abortions.

65. Trump imposed sanctions on the socialists in Venezuela who have killed their citizens.

66. Finalized new trade agreement with South Korea.

67. Made a deal with the European Union to increase U.S. energy exports to Europe.

68. Withdrew the U.S. from the job killing TPP deal.

69. Secured $250 billion in new trade and investment deals in China and $12 billion in Vietnam.

70. Okayed up to $12 billion in aid for farmers affected by unfair trade retaliation.

71. Has had over a dozen US hostages freed.

72. Trump signed the Music Modernization Act, the biggest change to copyright law in decades.

73. Trump secured billions that will fund the building of a wall at our southern border.

74. The Trump Administration is promoting second chance hiring to give former inmates the opportunity to live crime-free lives and find meaningful employment.

75. Trump's DOJ and the Board of Prisons launched a new "Ready to Work Initiative" to help connect employers directly with former prisoners.

76. President Trump's historic tax cut legislation included new Opportunity Zone Incentives to promote investment in low-income communities across the country.

77. 8,764 communities across the country have been designated as Opportunity Zones.

78. Opportunity Zones are expected to spur $100 billion in long-term private capital investment in economically distressed communities across the country.

79. Trump directed the Education Secretary to end Common Core.

80. Trump signed the 9/11 Victims Compensation Fund into law.

81. Trump signed measure funding prevention programs for Veteran suicide.

82. Companies have brought back over a TRILLION dollars from overseas because of the TCJA bill that Trump signed.

83. [Prior to the coronavirus pandemic] manufacturing jobs were growing at the fastest rate in more than 30 years.

84. [Prior to the coronavirus pandemic] the stock market reached record highs.

85. [Prior to the coronavirus pandemic] Median household income hit highest level ever recorded.

86. [Prior to the coronavirus pandemic] African American unemployment is at an all-time low.

87. [Prior to the coronavirus pandemic] Hispanic-American unemployment is at an all-time low.

88. [Prior to the coronavirus pandemic] Asian-American unemployment is at an all-time low.

89. [Prior to the coronavirus pandemic] women's unemployment rate was at a 65-year low.

90. [Prior to the coronavirus pandemic] Youth unemployment is at a 50-year low.

91. [Prior to the coronavirus pandemic] We had the lowest unemployment rate ever recorded.

92. The Pledge to America's Workers has resulted in employers committing to train more than 4 million Americans.

93. [Prior to the coronavirus pandemic] 95 percent of U.S. manufacturers are optimistic about the future— the highest ever.

94. [Prior to the coronavirus pandemic] As a result of the Republican tax bill, small businesses will have the lowest top marginal tax rate in more than 80 years.

95. Record number of regulations eliminated that hurt small businesses.

96. Signed welfare reform requiring able-bodied adults who don't have children to work or look for work if they're on welfare.

97. Under Trump, the FDA approved more affordable generic drugs than ever before in history.

98. Reformed Medicare program to stop hospitals from overcharging low-income seniors on their drugs—saving seniors 100's of millions of $$$ this year alone.

99. Signed Right-To-Try legislation allowing terminally ill patients to try experimental treatment that wasn't allowed before.

100. Secured $6 billion in new funding to fight the opioid epidemic.

101. Signed VA Choice Act and VA Accountability Act, expanded VA telehealth services, walk-in-clinics, and same-day urgent primary and mental health care.
102. U.S. oil production recently reached all-time high, so we are less dependent on oil from the Middle East.
103. The U.S. is a net natural gas exporter for the first time since 1957.
104. NATO allies increased their defense spending because of his pressure campaign.
105. Withdrew the United States from the job-killing Paris Climate Accord in 2017 and that same year the U.S. still led the world by having the largest reduction in Carbon emissions.
106. Has his circuit court judge nominees being confirmed faster than any other new administration.
107. Had his Supreme Court Justice's Neil Gorsuch and Brett Kavanaugh confirmed.
108. Moved U.S. Embassy in Israel to Jerusalem.
109. Agreed to a new trade deal with Mexico & Canada that will increase jobs here and $$$ coming in.
110. Reached a breakthrough agreement with the E.U. to increase U.S. exports.
111. Imposed tariffs on China in response to China's forced technology transfer, intellectual property theft, and their chronically abusive trade practices, has agreed to a Part One trade deal with China.
112. Signed legislation to improve the National Suicide Hotline.
113. Signed the most comprehensive childhood cancer legislation ever into law, which will advance childhood cancer research and improve treatments.
114. The Tax Cuts and Jobs Act signed into law by Trump doubled the maximum amount of the child tax credit available to parents and lifted the income limits so more people could claim it.
115. It also created a new tax credit for other dependents.
116. In 2018, President Trump signed into law a $2.4 billion funding increase for the Child Care and Development Fund, providing a total of $8.1 billion to States to fund childcare for low-income families.

117. The Child and Dependent Care Tax Credit (CDCTC) signed into law by Trump provides a tax credit equal to 20-35% of child care expenses, $3,000 per child & $6,000 per family + Flexible Spending Accounts (FSAs) allow you to set aside up to $5,000 in pre-tax $ to use for child care.

118. In 2019 President Donald Trump signed the Autism Collaboration, Accountability, Research, Education and Support Act (CARES) into law which allocates $1.8 billion in funding over the next five years to help people with autism spectrum disorder and to help their families.

119. In 2019 President Trump signed into law two funding packages providing nearly $19 million in new funding for Lupus specific research and education programs, as well an additional $41.7 billion in funding for the National Institutes of Health (NIH), the most Lupus funding EVER.

Let me be clear with what was just shared. This is not a "Pro-Trump" play here. Ask yourself a question. Did this positive run through bullets anger you? For America to Heal we can no longer allow the praising of political officials we do not align with to be silenced. We should be able to allow for that across partisan lines. This is the result of effectively healing. President Trump makes it easy to judge him, because he wears most of his sins on the outside and to be politically correct, we the citizens of America suggest people should wear their sins on the inside. No one knows our sins. We wear out sins on the inside, hidden from the public eye. We know Donald J. Trump's sins. What if God placed Donald J. Trump in this position just to see who would judge him? What if one day that is revealed to us? How many stones have you thrown? Are you not in a glass house today? We hold leadership to a higher standard, but God will hold most to the same standard and only hold the leaders in the Church to a higher standard. With that said, I am not here to judge the president's moral character, but to engage our minds to consider "research" to see the good in everything and sometimes good can come from the most un-desired individuals or desired. Good cannot be defined by political ideology and or discounted by political ideology. Dennis Prager has often said, nothing good comes from the left. Because we are at "War" politically, then this is simply strategy I would hope and not an intelligent perceived conviction that the left and liberals hold no good. Diversity is always stronger. Diversity has made America strong and not just from conservative thought. A liberated thought was the original driver for Americans. With that said I am simply covering the positive facts of his Trump's presidency. In the bible the books of 1 and 2 Chronicles only captures the positives of the Kings of Israel and none of the negatives. The story of David and Bathsheba is not captured in the books of 1 or 2 Chronicles. If you want to know the negatives you will have to go to the books 1 Kings and II Kings. What does this mean. The book of Chronicles is only the good report of the Kings. Hopefully on judgement day God only reveals our good report and says "servant" well done. In the book of Malachi in the bible it says that God will have a book of remembrance and so the book of Chronicles is very similar to a book of remembrance by God. For example in Malachi 3:16-17 NIV [16]Then those who feared the LORD talked with each other, and the LORD listened and heard. A scroll of remembrance was written in his presence concerning those who feared the LORD and honored his name. [17]"On the day when I act," says the LORD Almighty, "they will be my treasured possession. I will spare them, just as a father has compassion and spares his son who serves him. Even God can forgive our negatives, blotch them out, and remember our good. Christians should be able to do the same. I would do the same for Obama as well. Has Donald Trump done anything good? I believe we can say, "yes" he has if we are being honest. Then why is he perceived to be a threat so often by certain news cast and the left public? The answer is mainly Donald Trump doesn't feel the need to address the perceptions about his character. Like me I gave so much to my team at work as you can recall in the Chapter Perception is Reality. It didn't matter how much good I did for my team; it was not effective due to their perception of me. A privileged posture will not allow a person to be humble enough to address perceptions. Can we allow for any growth in our feelings towards Donald Trump outside of our personal perceptions and let me not down-play raw facts as well? To grow, it may require us to be uncomfortable about even saying something good about Donald Trump. It may require the right to say something good about Joe Biden. Perceptions on Donald Trump are strong, and we know he does not have the ability to nurture, but he has delivered some good. So why then are we still desiring some nurturing there. It is natural, that's why. It is "Natural" to desire nurturing from leadership. Absence of that nurturing can be unsettling and then harm trust in that relationship with the leader.

Joe Biden may very well have the ability to nurture. Joe Biden may have the ability to unite this country, if the attitudes are open to it. Can Joe sustain the momentum of the current economy and grow us from there? Is there something Joe Biden can learn from Donald Trump? Was there something Donald Trump could learn from Obama? All of these answers must eventually be a sound "yes" with a good spirit about it. Honor good accomplishments even by those you disagree with. This seed helps the healing process. It removes the edge.

Our current economy is the strongest it has been, possibly ever. We have become a country of exports and making money instead of the country of imports and money was leaving. Trade deals and the financial margins coming back to the United States have all been improved. This was what has been recorded as the meaning behind "Make America Great Again" and not the message most may have believed, which was a knock on Barack Obama, a knock on liberals, and to also mean "Let's Make America White Again". Much of it I am willing to say or probably not as true as we believe. We are so polarized in America today, that even the subtle punch is magnified to become a knockout swing for the people that desire vindication. "Make America Great Again" was that a knockout swing of vindication. It was received with the uppermost offense. So, then it began. Fight! Fight! Fight!

For others these bullets outlining Donald Trump's accomplishments will be celebrated and then others it will turn just the opposite and possibly land me in the demonized zones as well. We must begin to not so quickly see anyone American as a significant threat to America, but simply learned and unlearned. We must be willing to nurture the unlearned and help with understanding. Nurturing each other is not entirely the president's responsibility. We must love our neighbors as well. We should be able to speak well of candidates without hostility, without fear of being non-partisan, and without fear of being demonized for simply recognizing the good in everyone. In 2008 Senator John McCain defended Obama, his opponent in the election when a woman called Obama some nasty names in an open discussion forum. John McCain interrupted her and took the microphone from her and outspokenly disagreed with her statement. The Senator then stated that Obama was a respectable family man, and decent person. John McCain went on to say that he simply has fundamental disagreements with Obama. Where is that spirit today in America? Can a democrat not openly say that Donald Trump has greatly improved the performance of America's Economy without being demonized? I believe we know in our hearts where it has gone, and we know why. Attitudes will often reflect leadership. Let us "Heal America". No fear here in what was shared. Learn, Love, and then Let Go.

A "healed" people, will be begin to hear differently. We must grow to a place in American where it is safe for Citizens and Politicians to be bipartisan to the open public without fear of being cast out by their party. Let us begin to create that type of atmosphere without bullying those individuals. American has become overly partisan and then overly reactive to everything outside of the political ideologies they have signed up with. Let's pivot with the sincere desire to setup an open dialogue of bi-partisan conversations with no bullying from either side. Love, sacrifice, and services to one another, so we heal. Heal America.

What does God have to say: Understanding Brings Peace

> Whoever derides their neighbor has no sense, but the one who has understanding holds their tongue. (Proverbs 11:12 NIV)

Silence is recommended here as an instance of true friendship—and a preservative of it—and it is evidence of wisdom. A person of understanding has rule over their spirit. If they are provoked, they hold their peace and neither vent to his passion nor kindle the passion of others by any opprobrious language or peevish reflections. The person with a faithful spirit is true to their own promise and to the interest of their friends. They conceal every matter that, if divulged, could turn to the prejudice of their neighbor:

> Do not rebuke mockers or they will hate you; rebuke the wise and they will love you. (Proverbs 9:8 NIV)

> Not many of you should become teachers, my fellow believers, because you know that we who teach will be judged more strictly. We all stumble in many ways. Anyone who is never at fault in what they say is perfect, able to keep their whole body in check.

> When we put bits into the mouths of horses to make them obey us, we can turn the whole animal. Or take ships as an example. Although they are so large and are driven by strong winds, they are steered by a very small rudder wherever the pilot wants to go. Likewise, the tongue is a small part of the body, but it makes great boasts. Consider what a great forest is set on fire by a small spark. The tongue also is a fire, a world of evil among the parts of the body. It corrupts the whole body, sets the whole course of one's life on fire, and is itself set on fire by hell.

> All kinds of animals, birds, reptiles, and sea creatures are being tamed and have been tamed by mankind, but no

human being can tame the tongue. It is a restless evil, full of deadly poison.

With the tongue we praise our Lord and Father, and with it we curse human beings, who have been made in God's likeness. Out of the same mouth come praise and cursing. My brothers and sisters, this should not be. Can both fresh water and salt-water flow from the same spring? My brothers and sisters, can a fig tree bear olives, or a grapevine bear figs? Neither can a salt spring produce fresh water. (James 3:1–12 NIV)

We must know our audiences. Effective communication is better than just communication.

SIX

THE DESIRE FOR VINDICATION

Chapters 4, 5, and 6 examine the causes of pain in America. One of the significant pain triggers is the desire to be vindicated. If we revisit the situation with Jammer in Chapter 1, we can remember that his Boss was helping to escalate a strong desire to be vindicated and or to be treated justly. Many are in those shoes today that Jammer was in that day. There is something or someone close by encouraging that same desire to be vindicated. This does not mean a man or woman should not desire to be treated fairly or to obtain justice, but vindication can be become a sin if it is over indulged in. Christians have been given a pardon, by God. This pardon by God allows us to not receive something we deserved in this earthly realm while still having hope of what has been promised to us in the spiritual realm, Heaven. We call it mercy. Isaiah 54:7-8 NIV [7]"For a brief moment I abandoned you, but with deep compassion I will bring you back. [8]In a surge of anger I hid my face from you for a moment, but with everlasting kindness I will have compassion on you," says the LORD your Redeemer. Vindication can become a sin if it starts to consume us. Shouldn't we learn mercy unto others as well? We have heard no justice, no peace. Justice will sometimes be in God's hands and because of that we are able to have peace. As Christians we are never without peace, if we are living spiritual. Pride can be one of the drivers behind vindication. For Christians, the Word of God says that he hates pride.

I attended a church men's retreat, and it was the first time I convinced my dad to go with me. I had hoped the trip would be a moment of healing for us because we had not spent quality time together. In 2009, my dad and I had some differences with each other, and I believed he was wrong. There was also some tension between the minister of the church and some of the young adult facilitators in the church, which I was a part of. I sent an email to the young adult group to share an inspirational devotional from an author who was not of any religious background. He spoke about how people respond better to an outside voice than to the voices that are close to them. I sent the email to the young adult group, and the minister of the church sent an email out to the same distribution list, asking me not to share items with the young adults outside of the Gospel being preached.

I felt embarrassed. Reprimanding me in front of the group I volunteered to lead was not right. I shared the issue with my dad and this minister with the speaker who was facilitating the retreat. The speaker listened to me several times, and each time, he tried to share something with me that was positive and from a perspective of peace and love.

What I felt in my heart was that my dad had been wrong about some things he was pressuring me with—and the minister was wrong about how he handled the email I sent out. I felt I was owed an apology and that they both should own up to the wrong they had done.

The conversation took place during one of the fifteen-minute health breaks. The speaker looked at me directly and said the most massive words I had ever been hit with. I still have not forgotten his words. His words humbled me beyond measure, and I finally realized how blind I had been through the conflicts. He said, "Who are you that you feel you need to be vindicated?"

Whoa! Whoa! I sat down, and a few of the other young adult organizers looked at my body language and facial expression. I was struck. These were just words, but they cut like a double edge sword. I felt what he said to my core and it pricked my heart. I sat down and thought, *How right he was.* My ego or superego had gotten the best of me again and I had a strong desire to be right. To dominate. To control. To be justified. I felt like I should be vindicated, and my dad and the minister had not offered any apology to me. What was I, to feel they owed me that? What arrogance. These two men had done so much for me as a person and helped mentor and grow me into the man I was, and I reached a point with them that when they wronged me, I desired to be made whole by them. I thought of how many times in my life the conflict lasted longer than it should have because I had this strong desire to be vindicated and made whole through another man being wrong towards me. No mercy and no forgiveness towards the people that help to grow me to the man I am today. I wanted to leave out of this men's retreat and go back to my room and somber for a while from the shame and failure I was feeling inside.

A strong desire to be vindicated can eventually make one vindictive. Vindication is proving that what someone said or did was right or true after other people thought it was wrong. It is proof that someone or something is right, reasonable, or justified. Many Americans suffer from a strong desire to be vindicated. This desire is like a virus that erupts from the pride boiling over inside until the temperature of unrest finally shouts out in bursting flames, "You are wrong! Now, you owe me something."

So much harm and pain come from waiting on an opportunity for vindication, which may not come. If someone makes a statement that is insulting or offensive to us, we troll the person until we can post back— and then we can feel vindicated. If there was a unkept promise in the political platform of a candidate, the desire to be vindicated is like a wedge in the progress of the decisions being made possible for the greater public good. This desire births anger, irritability, and an abrasive posture toward our neighbors. Vindication should not be a bad word. It can be a bad word when it is the driver of behaviors that do not resolve the conflict, but instead prolong it. Why did I think so highly of myself that I deserved or had earned the right to be vindicated? This does not mean you just get walked on by the opposite faction, but you become humble to the point where the actions of others do not define you or hold power over you.

Today's political climate is warring with the desire to be vindicated. Each side wants vindication. Much pain has come from this driver of the hard cuts in society. You can see the ugly side of America in the responses to political posts. Since I cannot gain vindication, I can gain some small amount of vindication by insulting you or belittling you. How do we grow as a nation if we do not come to terms with this virus that has plagued us? You wronged me—and now you owe me something. Confess to it!

The speaker at the men's retreat was trying to reveal my arrogance and how the ego had taken over me with a desire to be vindicated. I expected to be right. In humility and during the process of chewing on this statement, I thought, *"Who am I that I have a need to be vindicated?" Have you become tied to this desire that a relationship with your father and the minister no longer matter and are undervalued because the desire to be right is greater?*

The answer was subtle. *No. I do not want to be that guy any longer—not today. I don't want to be that guy ever again.* It felt shameful, and I could not believe I had fallen into it. One of the significant pains in America today is the desire to be vindicated. We suffer with it in social media, in the news, and even with daily dialogue. The news agendas are plagued with it as well. "Because a man was wrong, he owes me something."

It's not to say a person should not gain justice or receive vindication, but the desire for it could have become sin or a flaw. Awareness of the enemy is half the battle. I ask that we agree that this has been a sleeper in terms of an opponent in the game of healing. In many cases, this desire to be vindicated has been yielded by the entitlement theory that seems to have surfaced as a generational virus. I would have to say the previous generation of parents should humbly own this challenge that has categorized a nation of youth and young adults. One other strong thought on this entitlement theory is the absence or limited presence of a grateful heart. Not being grateful will prevent a person from feeling joy of any sort.

The current generation can be blind to the prosperity around us. This could be a direct result of being identified as the participation trophy generation or the entitled generation. The daily news feed on our phones showcase the latest headlines of presidential candidates calling for policies to fix the so-called injustices of capitalism in the US. If we put down our phones for a few minutes and just look around, we'll see the prosperity of living in a nation that offers the liberties of free opportunities all around us.

At Starbucks, you might see people talking freely, working on their MacBooks, ordering food they get in an instant, and seeing cars go by outside. Is this the fruit of capitalism? We live in the most privileged time, in the most prosperous nation, and have the greatest benefits. Have we lost sight of what we should be truly grateful for? Has a new generation not seen this as having any value? Vehicles, food, technology, and the freedom to associate with whom you choose are so ingrained in the American way of life that we don't give them a second thought. This is also privilege, and it does not have a race that defines it. This generation has not confessed to it. We are so blessed here in the United States that our poverty line begins significantly higher than the global average—thirty-one times higher to be exact.

No one in the United States is considered poor by a global review. We live in an era where we can order a product off Amazon with one click and have it delivered to our doorstep the very next day—almost less than twenty-four hours after the purchase. Have we become unappreciative, unsatisfied, and ungrateful about the liberties and privileges that capitalism has yielded?

Our unappreciation becomes more and more evident as the popularity of socialist policies among the current generation continues to grow. Congresswoman Alexandria Ocasio-Cortez recently talked to a *Newsweek* journalist about the millennial generation. "An entire generation, which is now becoming one of the largest electorates in America, came of age and never saw American prosperity." With a bartender's salary in New York, life can be challenging. I understand where some of this is coming from, but there is a larger nation of beneficiaries to the capitalism we have in place. It's bigger than the challenges of the cost of living in New York.

Many people share this perception that AOC is suggesting. Is it a fact for everyone or just those in certain regions under certain circumstances? This current generation is being indoctrinated by a mainstream narrative that is being materialized as a righteous movement to help everyone succeed, but it will eventually reduce the efforts of them to do their best and plan for their success. To believe we have never seen prosperity is not a true statement by any popular group. I know this firsthand. I went to college, I had a car, I had a job, I had extra money, I traveled, and I had great experiences. Does that make me privileged and separated from the realities of others? It does, but it also means I have seen prosperity and negates that it doesn't exist.

With all the overwhelming evidence around us—proof that one can see from a coffee shop—why don't we all view this as prosperity? We have people who are dying to get into our country. At the border in Texas, they are directly breaking the laws of our country for a chance to live here. They are risking being separated from their children because it is a better life to be locked up here than back home where they are running from. They want a shot at the liberties we take for granted.

People around the world are destitute and truly impoverished. We may have a young generation convinced they've never seen prosperity, and as a result, a politician with a different experience could be convinced about strategies toward abolishing capitalism. Capitalism is not the enemy. Being balanced and good-hearted at times is more or less the enemy. This current generation did not live through the Great Depression or two world wars, the Korean War, the Vietnam War, or even see the rise and fall of socialism and communism. There are historical areas they are not fully aware of.

This current generation doesn't know what it's like to live without the internet, without cars, or without smartphones. It would be difficult to say that America has a lack of prosperity problem, but we might have an entitlement problem and an ungratefulness problem that is spreading like a plague. I say this with all due respect for the current generation, and our lives will be in your hands one day. We want you to be educated on it all and always consider the full scope of your thoughts to go beyond the current pain you feel. Learn from history, grow in long-term understanding, and refrain from trying to solve adversity with limited data.

Can a sense of entitlement drive vindication? Let me start by saying

I have nothing against AOC. I admire her drive and courage. I simply want to examine this transparency of a college student's perspective or perception of the subject. This is part of trying to understand. Is this an absolute? Maybe, maybe not. For sure, there is much validity and realness to what was stated.

AOC has some strong views. I had a boss once who advised me not to ever come across as a threat if I wanted to gain others' confidence in me. This meant adjusting my tone and posture while communicating strong ideas and views. This boss told me that nothing is ever wrong with my intentions, but a friendlier tone is desired to be listened to and not just heard. I believe AOC does not see herself perceived as a threat but an advancement or shift in solutions for all Americans. Perception is reality. They must ask themselves how they are perceived to understand how many will respond. A sense of entitlement can make one feel the need to be vindicated. Is vindication a problem in America? Would one be blind to be grateful if they strongly desired to be vindicated? I believe that is possible. A thankful heart is blocked by a posture to be reconciled for wrongdoings toward us.

Let us consider vindication when it comes to positives. The civil rights movement was positive in terms of the desire to be vindicated. Women's rights were positive in terms of the desire to be vindicated as well. The desire to be vindicated is not always malicious or bad. Donald Trump desired to be vindicated after the Mueller investigation was completed. Sometimes the desire to be vindicated is simply holding someone to be just and honest about a situation. America has a struggle with that today.

The Black Lives Matter movement desires to be vindicated on the subject of police brutality. Cops are being demonized in the process of the desire to be protected. This is a tough spot to be in, and we must first understand the culture of the police in America and lead by respecting that. Many people would say we are past the point of respect. If this is a truth, then we are yielding to something significant to accomplish this vindication. This is not bad, but we must sometimes understand the season we are in. This is our season. If we want to heal, we must be patient. We must love. We must display empathy. If we want to heal, we have to listen. We have to be willing not to be fearful of our own culture and losing some ground. It's uncomfortable, but if we want to grow, we will have to go there. One of the leading causes of a desire to be vindicated, turning into something more harmful than a positive, is when it is fueled by pride. Pride is a sin:

> Pride goes before destruction, a haughty spirit
> before a fall. (Proverbs 16:18 NIV)

Pride does not allow us to listen, feel empathy, or compromise. If we consider Colin Kaepernick, the kneeling for the flag controversy, and the subject being protested around police brutality, we can see where culture is the main issue in the adversity against Kaepernick. The flag is significant in culture, and police are significant in culture. This becomes a double whammy. Both sides begin to desire to be "vindicated." Both sides hurt.

Pride sets in, and we are in an unstable situation that is making more wounds every day. Is this the Rosa Parks move of the new millennium? Will this be the benchmark of awareness? Is this an attack on a culture? Where we stand in this moment is a measurement of what we idealize today on the subject of country, flag, military, cops. There is one perception, and it becomes a reality.

The other perception is that you don't care about us, and we are getting unjustly killed. Is humanity greater—or is culture greater? Culture is heavily weighted and very strong even though it should never outweigh the value of humanity. None of this is the problem. Pride is the enemy, and a desire to be vindicated dwells on both sides.

I do not want to minimize the movement and what Kaepernick is pleading for. I also do not want to reduce the culture that has been prevalent in these subjects since the beginning of America's first war. For us to heal, we have to bring it all to the table, honor what needs to be honored, and then speak about the issues respectfully. If something is perceived as disrespectful, then you have minimized the audience, which might have been willing to help. Culture is big. Respect is big. Perception is reality. Tie it all together, and we gain an understanding of how to be effective in our approaches. Honor your audience first, show respect, and then begin your protest respectfully. If that does not work, take the next steps in action. This is no coaching to Kaepernick, but sharing alternatives to the approach could be more effective. Vindication, if not balanced and without pride, can be a sin. Vindication in love for the greater good can be a blessing that lasts a lifetime.

I want us to consider how the families of police officers feel during times of unrest and contention toward law enforcement. Imagine how difficult it might be for them to do their jobs safely today? An officer shared some of his experiences during his time serving the public. He stated how he had pulled dead, mangled bodies from cars, lied to people as they were dying, and told them they were going to be fine as he held their hands and watched the life fade out. Imagine holding dying babies, buying lunch for people who were mentally ill, and not eating in a while with money that was for your own family?

Officers have been attacked and have had people try to stab them or shoot them. I have heard reports on domestic cases, which are the most dangerous police house calls, being attacked by women while they were arresting their husbands who had just severely beaten them. Some in law enforcement have bullet wounds or have held towels on other officers' bullet wounds.

Officers can share incidents when they had to administer CPR when they knew it wouldn't help just to make family members feel better about their efforts. Law enforcement has had to break down doors, fight in drug houses, chase fugitives through the woods, and think the whole time, *This might be it.* We all have witnessed high-speed car chases on the news and breaking news events from time to time, and sometimes these turn into foot chases across interstates during rush hour. Police officers have been in crashes and squeezed the trigger—about to kill a man—before they come to their senses, stop themselves, and conquer their adrenaline. There are instances where an officer must navigate through angry crowds to sort out chaos. There are moments when a patrolman might let little kids who don't have much sit in their patrol car and pretend they are a cop for their birthday. The number of those who are taken to jail do not always outweigh the number who are given breaks. We have seen videos of officers who are spiritually grounded praying for people they don't even know. Officers have the challenging decision to decide when to be violent when they have to be and when to be kind.

I have heard of officers separating themselves to cry about an experience when it overwhelmed them. Law enforcement will tell you that they have missed Christmas and other holidays more than they wanted to. Every cop I know has done all these things and more for lousy pay, exhausting hours, and a short life expectancy. I do not believe they deserve our pity or even desire it because it is what they signed up for, but I do believe we can show some empathy towards them.

There are unique fears on both sides, and the majority do not have issues with either side, but lives are being affected by a minority of bad actors. In corporate America, rules are put in place for less than 10 percent of abusers, and more than 90 percent have to adhere to them. Political propaganda drives narratives of a few, and a majority has to listen to it. Political news correspondents need material to drive narratives to sway votes and play on the fears and emotions of the population. If we start to attack the cultures of it all, then cultures will realign, votes will realign, and there will be no progress but additional pains. Law enforcement is a part of a strong culture in America. When we attack law enforcement, we are attacking culture. We must learn that anytime we are attacking culture, we are going to get a fight. In the end, there will be no winners when culture is involved. It will become a vicious cycle of harm. What are the alternatives? We are making threats toward a law enforcement culture based on less than 10 percent of the group—just as a corporate structure would do. Let us be careful. Should 90 percent get the blame for what 10 percent are doing?

Love transcends all. Let us approach this in love. We must listen, we must show respect, and we must agree to respond with an unbiased care for humanity. Historically, the police are part of noble society. This has not been dissolved due to the cases that are negatively affecting that image today. Each person has a different reality.

There is a view on prosperity, capitalism, law enforcement, unarmed Black men, and African Americans. Each person has a perception and historical support for their perceptions. Consider those who are four or five generations from slavery. Their great-great-grandfathers were slaves, and their current family names come from the original slave master. The thought of this history can be painful.

Many slaves were greatly abused, starved, sold, and later called lazy if they were not working toward the expectations of their master. Slaves were treated inappropriately. If a slave ran away and was captured, the punishment was very bad. It was not limited to a beating; there was also cutting off life and limb to discipline.

Once the slaves were freed, the torture did not end. Emancipated slaves could often be subject to White men who would put on sheets and raid their homes, rape their wives, and lynch those outside of the law for simply looking eye to eye with a White man. This was perceived as great disrespect.

When former slaves separated themselves into their own thriving communities in Tulsa, Rosewood, Mound Bayou, Colfax, and Atlanta, the communities were destroyed for no reason other than envy or jealousy. These freed slave communities suffered bombings, burning of their homes, vandalizing of their businesses, brutalizing of the men, and dehumanizing of strong members of each family. Even where an African American sat on a bus was an issue. They were forced to stand up, and if they were not fast enough, they were often dragged off the buses, off the streets, out of restaurants, out of businesses, and out of their own homes.

When African Americans marched peacefully, unarmed, the national guard, fire hoses, and dogs were used. African American churches were bombed, and leaders were assassinated. As we advance these historical treatments to the events that are hot items today, we might see why they are so quickly magnified. It is mainly due to a history of similarities.

While current perceptions should be free and clear of the past, they are not. The past is very relevant and still has a strong hold in the perceptions of today. When African Americans kneeled in peaceful protest, no one desired to address the issue behind the kneeling. The lesser road was taken, and that was to simply rewrite the narrative, add a political view to it, and dehumanize the gesture as unpatriotic. They were told to stand and "drag them out" of that kneel. Does this sound familiar?

As they protested, it was perceived as disrespect. I share this not to make anyone feel guilty or ashamed but to bring insight to the nature of the posture and perception. If we address the perception, we can help the healing. In all the years of peaceful protest and demonstrations, the historical label has always been that the actions of African Americans were "inappropriate."

In addition to the years of rebelling, fighting, and protesting, America has never publicly acknowledged a changed behavior should be considered on the more painful topics that our nation faces. The perception and the reality are both that unarmed African Americans are being killed by law enforcement and the examples are becoming more and more frequent. With these incidents happening, it is not empathetic to coach African Americans on how to respond to the pain. We can help each other heal by listening and responding without a political narrative driving the response of love and care.

There are two perceptions and two realities. In the arena of vindication, there is rarely a winner. The guarantee in most cases is there will be two enemies. What is the driver in both of these writings? The driver is a desire to be justified. It is not always a negative, and in unique cases, it is just a wish to be heard. Communication is a huge key, and relationships must be formed to reconcile the perspectives to a common ground of peace. Listen to each other. Genuinely listen and then trade shoes. Show empathy. In most cases, the parties both want the same goal and have no issues with the stance of the other. They just have problems with the aggressive, harmful culprits of fear.

In many cases, the pressures are coming from outside sources that are independent of those closest to you on social media, coworkers, or associates. Can we identify two separate pains here? Maybe three? Can we believe that neither would have an issue with the other after a conversation? Pride and vindication, in many cases, will not allow that to happen. God desires us to be orderly with each other and show some love and compassion. It is difficult when the majority of the public seems not to be listening.

Listening is the launch pad for trust. Trust will not have its day without sincerely listening:

> But I said, "I have labored in vain; I have spent my strength
> for nothing at all. Yet what is due me is in the Lord's hand,
> and my reward is with my God." (Isaiah 49:4 NIV)

The continuous desire to be right and make sure everyone knows we are right is a disease that social media spreads like a plague. *If I just clarify one more time,* I think, *if I apply one more argument, I will be seen as right.* This is not the same as carrying on a long and spirited discussion. In fact, this is a sin nobody can judge as existing in anyone but themselves.

Externally, the person seeking truth will look like the person seeking vindication, but the outcome in the soul is utterly different. If we seek vindication, we love reputation and not the truth, but only we will know. God, help us know when we have made this error. When I am wronged, my immediate reaction is to wish for vindication, but then I remember the mercy I have received and the pity I need in my life.

There is nothing wrong with wanting God to be vindicated. Goodness should be thought of as good, the truth should be known to be true, and beauty should be perceived as beautiful. As far as we know, God and the holy angels are the only ones who can cry only for justice and not for mercy, yet the angels do not ask for justice for themselves. Why not?

If God is given justice, then all the just will flourish:

> See what this godly sorrow has produced in you: what earnestness, what eagerness to clear yourselves, what indignation, what alarm, what longing, what concern, what readiness to see justice done. At every point you have proved yourselves to be innocent in this matter. (2 Corinthians 7:11 NIV)

They do not wish for personal vindication—but for good to be vindicated. I join those who cry for mercy, and this is incompatible with living a life that is centered on personal vindication. The lust for personal vindication is a sin rarely considered because we should wish for the right to prevail. We never wish error to triumph, but the subtle distinction that breeds error in our hearts makes us care less about justice than about appearing to be just.

Plato had it right: the reasonable person will love justice, even if their love of justice is perceived to be unjust. There is such an easy line between loving goodness, truth, and beauty and loving being perceived as good, true, and beautiful.

Love in Action

Love must be sincere. Hate what is evil; cling to what is good. Be devoted to one another in love. Honor one another above yourselves. Never be lacking in zeal, but keep your spiritual fervor, serving the Lord.

Be joyful in hope, patient in affliction, faithful in prayer. Share with the Lord's people who are in need. Practice hospitality.

Bless those who persecute you; bless and do not curse. Rejoice with those who rejoice; mourn with those who mourn. Live in harmony with one another. Do not be proud, but be willing to associate with people of low position. Do not be conceited.

Do not repay anyone evil for evil. Be careful to do what is right in the eyes of everyone. If it is possible, as far as it depends on you, live at peace with everyone. Do not take revenge, my dear friends, but leave room for God's wrath, for it is written: "It is mine to avenge; I will repay," says the Lord. (Romans 12:9–19 NIV)

Section 2 - Social Challenge

Identify your negative, that does not allow America to be great or you to feel great about America. What are you ashamed of? This takes courage to share, and it also takes humility. Share on Social Media and ask for forgiveness. Make it public. Then post what steps you will take to work on those areas of your life, to become a better citizen, teammate, friend, family member, employee, church member, or neighbor. Being humble is one of the most potent characteristics one can have. We must show it. This is not a shaming exercise, but a liberating exercise to set you free of things that we are not happy with about ourselves. How can I become more patriotic about the country I live in. Example: *(For me I owned nothing with an American Flag on it. I went and bought a hat, a flag, a shirt all with an American Flag on it. I wear them and post it on social media to show pride and patriotism.)*

SECTION III

THE SOLUTION

SEVEN

THE POWER IN
RELATIONSHIPS

In the next three chapters we will examine the possible solutions that could lead to healing in America. One very powerful approach is to focus on relationships with the opposition. Americans are not born to be threats to Americans. We are manipulated, stimulated, and encouraged to become threats to each other. The Elephant and Donkey say to the Lamb "Go Away". The Lamb speaks to holding others to a higher esteem than ourselves.

> "First Responders see the Relationship as the
> Greater Value than Their Views."

If we did, this then how could we hold any riff against our fellow American. Relationships are important. Once we elevate or expand our circle of friends to a more diverse group, we will see that we all have some of the same common denominators in mind for our lives. Then we can ask ourselves, if we both mostly want the same thing and I wish for you to be successful and you wish for me to be successful, then where is the contention. Sometimes the contention is simply a lack of personal accountability for one's own goals and in many cases, it is greater than that. The greater is mostly there is no relationship with the those we don't understand. Cultures we do not understand can lead us down a road to fear of that Culture's influence on my desired lifestyle and now an individual has very naturally assumed a threat. It can be that easy in becoming enemies, based on a perception. One strong solution to helping America Heal is to encourage more "First Responders". Remember the "First Responders" are those that do not respond. The First Responder has interest in the relationship, has matured in their emotions, and choose not to be offended. These 3 areas significantly reduce the media and political activist power of political propaganda.

> *Proverbs 9:8*
> *"Do not rebuke mockers or they will hate you;*
> *rebuke the wise and they will love you."*

I had a coworker, Bubbaloo, who I used to go to lunch with every Wednesday. We would go to a burger place that we both agreed was in our top three burger places in Houston. During the election of 2016, this coworker of mine—an ardent supporter of Donald Trump and a daily watcher of Fox News—thought it would be a good idea to share with me the progress America was going to make with Donald Trump as president.

Being African American, I found it very hard to listen to much of this conversation, but I would listen. On the day after the election, when he returned to work, I was no longer prepared to hear about Donald Trump. You see, when I woke up that morning, I had to somehow explain to my kids how Donald Trump won the presidency when the perception of him was that he was a racist.

I have three kids. Two of my kids are more into pop culture, and one is really into country music and has only dated White men who are into cowboy boots and country things. In my household, the feelings on the Donald Trump presidency win were sort of split. My daughter was not affected much by the win, and her social circle of friends was pro-Trump. My other two kids had a social circle of pop culture and were more liberated in thought, but conservative in spiritual areas.

Your social settings can soften your heart or lead your heart in directions that are different from how your household feels. Would this mean that most vote or align a certain way due to their social settings? There is a strong possibility. We conclude this decision as an absolute right decision in most cases. Is it? Peer pressure is strong, and social settings have a great deal of influence on how our perceptions align in this world today. This is one more reason why we have to examine our perceptions, adjust them to what is real, and dissolve what is not real from the negative impact on our lives and decision-making.

When Bubbaloo came into my office to celebrate the Trump victory, I asked my coworker to please leave my office. I told him that I didn't want to hear any Trump stories any longer. I was rude and very upset that he thought I would like to hear about it. For three or four months, we didn't speak much.

Bubbaloo started to come back around to my office and asked if he could come in each time, very politely. I told him he could, and we began to talk about things outside of politics. We started to go to lunch again together. After a year, we were reasonably back to normal. He even invited my wife and I over for a Christmas party with two other coworkers and their spouses. I believe I may have been the only person in the room who didn't vote for Donald Trump. We continued this tradition of coming together around the holidays to play games, sit around the fire, and enjoy wine, cheese, and beverages.

In the third year of our gathering, Bubbaloo's wife shared with us that he was adopted and did not have a good relationship with his mom. Bubbaloo was an army brat and had lived all over the world as a child. His adopted father was in the armed services, and he had a great deal of respect for America and a great deal of respect for the American flag. As you can imagine, we had some interesting conversations around the kneeling of the flag during sporting events. We both seemed to understand each other's point of view, but we still did not agree. Bubbaloo's wife continued to tell us about how his mom became jealous of his relationship with his father as he grew older.

Like me, Bubbaloo was an only child. I believe that is why we got along so well outside of politics. Bubbaloo's mother began pestering him and showing abrasive behavior toward him while his father was away. It made him very said and timid around his adopted mom. I had been friends now with Bubbaloo for five years and was unaware that he had been adopted. I assumed he had grown up as a privileged little White kid with everything one could imagine. Instead, he grew up with little and even a home that was unstable at times. He struggled to maintain friends due to always having to move and sometimes moved to another country. Bubbaloo settled down in Sugarland, Texas, after working as a salesman for many years and sent his kids to some of the best schools in the district.

By the end of the Christmas party, I had a newfound respect and admiration for Bubbaloo. I felt ashamed for kicking him out of my office because he was celebrating a Trump victory. I also felt ashamed that I had judged him as a person because of many stereotypes and profiles that affect our better judgement. As my wife and I were leaving the Christmas party, Bubbaloo was saying his goodbyes to all of us. When he got to me, he hugged me and told me that he loved me. I told him that I loved him as well. He then hugged my wife, and we all said, "I love you."

To be transparent, even though I was an only child, I didn't grow up in a household of affection. My parents rarely told me they loved me. They showed me they loved me all my life, but to say it was rare. Bubbaloo joined the handful of people in my life who had said I love you to me. Imagine that—from a Trump supporter and Fox news listener.

Beginning in about 2013, I began to understand that supporters of Donald Trump are not all racist, dumb, or bad people or any other stereotypes they have been given. You see, to believe this could be perceived as prejudice or racist as well. Let's correct that. Trump supporters are decent human beings and can be relied on to be good friends.

Today, Bubbaloo teaches me how to invest and prepare for retirement. We also talk about traveling and share experiences about places we have been. I consider him one of my closest friends, and he is ten years older than I am. Relationships are significant, and if diverse, they can help us grow in so many areas. Perceptions can be destroyed, and realities can be changed. It's all in the relationship if we want to conquer the perception. Do not shy away from it. Go towards it. Get to know people you are uncomfortable with knowing.

In 2013, I became a minister. I started school in 2012 while working at AT&T. I would go to class at night, and I had to turn in two sermon outlines per week in most modules. In 2013, I graduated and started preaching in the Church of Christ in Sugarland. I later did mission work in Guyana—in the same place where Jim Jones conducted his cult missions and caused the killing and suicides of several Americans and negatively affected the image of Guyana.

I got married in 2015, and my wife lived in Deer Park, Texas. Deer Park is believed to be the birthplace of Texas. In 2014, I told my soon-to-be wife that we should visit the Deer Park Church of Christ because it was closer to her home. On our first visit to Deer Park, we met the elders and were welcomed with a great show of hospitality. I am African American, and my wife is Mexican American. The Church of Christ in Deer Park is about 99 percent Caucasian. As we pulled into the parking lot, we saw a Trump bumper sticker. We did not think much of it because I already had seen some growth in my relationship with Bubbaloo. So, it was all good. I told the elders at Deer Park that I was a minister at the Church of Christ in Sugarland. The minister in Deer Park had been having some health issues, and he had been in and out of the hospital and was not able to consistently preach on Sundays.

On my third visit to Deer Park Church of Christ, I was asked if I could preach there the next Sunday due to their minister being ill. I told the elder that I needed to check with the Sugarland Church of Christ, and he informed me that he had already done that. I had been given a good report, and they said that Deer Park could use me—but could not try to recruit me.

We both chuckled, and the stage was set for me to preach at Deer Park. Deer Park is a conservative community in the suburbs of Houston, and many of the members are supporters of Trump. In 2020, I am still preaching at Deer Park. Since 2019, I have been the full-time interim minister there to the body of Christ with a great number of Trump supporters and mostly Caucasian conservatives.

In the six years at Deer Park, I have done community services with other members and even set up a neighborhood prayer tent. We serve meals for the men in a drug addiction recovery home at a local establishment called the Wheelhouse.

A Trump supporter is not an automatic racist, and relationships are everything for us to get past some of our insecurities about things we do not fully understand. We have not allowed ourselves to get out of our comfort zones to learn and get to know others with opposing views. Imagine an African American preaching at the congregation with mostly Trump supporters—conservatives or Republicans.

Relationships are the key to destroying perceptions. I have well-established relationships with individuals who were raised in completely different social settings than I was. Each of those relationships has added such great value and richness to my life. Let us grow through what we know. Step out of our comfort zone and meet and spend time with others who are not like you, and you will find out how much they are like you in the process.

A Beautiful Day in the Neighborhood was a great example of relationships, feelings, and pride. Lloyd Vogel was tasked with interviewing Mr. Rogers, and the interviewer quickly became the interviewee. Mr. Rogers, an ordained minister, was crafty about getting into people's hearts and minds to uncover their feelings and challenges. Lloyd Vogel suffered from something many Americans suffer from today, and that is pride. Mr. Rogers spent quality time with Lloyd and used his patient and nurturing nature to remedy the issues inside of Lloyd and encouraged him to mend things with his father before he passed away. Fred Rogers was not perfect, but he was transparent about his shortcomings in life.

One of the big takeaways from the movie was when Fred Rogers showed Lloyd Vogel the sign language for friendship. I believe this point in the film was significant and thoroughly explained Mr. Rogers's motive in what he was doing with Lloyd Vogel. He was working on a friendship with him without him knowing it. I believe Bubbaloo was doing the same with me.

I believe God does the same with us all as well. I challenge you to use the sign language for friendship on a daily basis to greet people. Use it more than hand waving. The sign language for friendship says we are neighbors and have a relationship with each other. It is no longer the ingenuine perception sometimes given by just a wave.

I encourage you to watch *A Beautiful Day in the Neighborhood* with your family or alone. It is powerful, and it will pivot your heart towards humanity and the focus on relationships. Mr. Fred Rogers was a humble and kind man who we can all learn from. Friends, friends, friends. If police officers approached scenes with the friendship sign language, people would respond with the same sign? Could that help defuse situations? What if we started a trend of doing that on a daily basis? Instead of waving at each other, we could give the sign for friendship. What if politicians greeted each other as such in the public eye. As part of the healing process, I want to challenge all Americans to begin to greet one another with the sign for friendship. Let this be our mantra now and approach to each other as friends.

Have you ever looked into a kaleidoscope? Do you remember playing with one as a kid? Do you realize that each person who looks into one would see different colors, shapes, and configurations? A kaleidoscope can also represent perspective. Everyone has their own perspective. It's made up of the breadth of their knowledge and experience. What they see could be based on their experiences in life. Each person could have a different reality in what they see in the kaleidoscope.

The languages of love and culture are created during our formative years. We all see things through that scope. Everything you think and know is based upon your unique perspective. For each race, culture, and upbringing, it can be different. Your perspective can change along with how you educate yourself, the social circles you keep, and the experiences and opportunities you have. The key to unity, prosperity, and peace within our incredibly diverse society is realizing that each person is looking through life in the lens of their own kaleidoscope.

What about engineering and science when it comes to relationships? Can they have a relationship with each other? Humans, under incredible research and discipline, have designed various life-improving technologies to accelerate the quality of living and advancement of experiences rendering a sense of the expected standard of today to conscious minds.

Today's advancements would have been seen as witchcraft in the 1600s or 1800s. Bluetooth is a wireless technology standard for exchanging data over short distances using short-wavelength UHF radio waves in the ISM band from 2.400 to 2.485 GHz from fixed and mobile devices and building personal area networks. The development of the "short-link" radio technology, later named Bluetooth, was initiated in 1989 by Nils Rydbeck, CTO at Ericsson Mobile in Lund, Sweden, and by Johan Ullman. The purpose was to develop wireless headsets. Today, who doesn't own some flavor of Bluetooth technology? It comes in speakers, headphones, stereo equipment, smart home technology, car radios, and GPS devices. Biomedical engineering originated two hundred years ago during the electrophysiology studies of Galvani and Volta. Biomedical engineers bridged the gap between engineering and medicine to form a relationship between both worlds and restore some normalcy to those affected by unfortunate situations, disease, and disasters. Relationships in science and engineering are critical.

In the twentieth century, biomedical engineering focused on tissue and cells' electrical properties, another form of relationship within our bodies. World War I and II saw the start of radiation therapy. Medical inventions helped in the development of improved diagnostic techniques and have led to the development of medicines for the treatment of some terminal diseases. A significant contribution of biomedical engineering is the design and development of medical devices that replace the body parts. These devices function in a relationship with the body. What is the point in all this? Relationships are powerful in any form and are essential to our advancement in any space.

Have you ever watched a spider spin its web? For days, during the stay-at-home COVID-19 Pandemic of 2020, I sat on the back porch in the evenings. I noticed a spider beginning to spin a web around six o'clock each evening. Apparently, spiders can tell time. It was very consistent with its starting time each day. God, can you explain this? By the time it was dark, the spider would have the web completed. It spun the web between the light drawstring and the ceiling fan blade drawstring on our back porch. It was the perfect spot to catch bugs in midair. Who taught this spider how to spin a web?

I began to pay attention to the birds in my backyard as they made nests in the oak trees. Who trained these birds? The nests and spider webs had the prettiest patterns. The spider does not get caught in his web. Animals have a relationship with God. Nature has a relationship with God. He is their trainer, and they do not challenge him.

I watched a "Shark Week" episode where they were stationed in Australia, and they were researching the killing of great White sharks. They were trying to find out what animal could be preying on them. The great white shark is the most feared predator in the ocean. The scientists set out to place trackers on several great white sharks with video on them to see if they were fortunate enough to catch a great white shark being attacked. Could it have been a cannibalistic attack by its own kind? e research finally showed that killer whales would come up from underneath a great white shark and bite the belly or liver area and then drive the great white shark out of the water and -flip it on its back. The great white's buoyancy is in its liver area, and it became paralyzed on its back. On its back, it was vulnerable and powerless. How did the Orca know this about the great white shark? They were trying to find out what animal could be preying on them. The great White shark is the most feared predator in the ocean. The scientists set out to place trackers on several great White sharks with video on them to see if they were fortunate enough to catch a great White shark being attacked. Could it have been a cannibalistic attack by its own kind? The research finally showed that killer whales would come up from underneath a great White shark and bite the belly or liver area and then drive the great White shark out of the water and flip it on its back. The great White's buoyancy is in its liver area, and it became paralyzed on its back. On its back, it was vulnerable and powerless. How did the orca know this about the great White shark?

Nature has a relationship with God. The scientists were astonished and awed by what they uncovered. Natural laws are hierarchical in nature; secondary laws of nature are based on primary laws of nature, which must be just right for our universe to be possible. Where did these laws come from? Why do they exist? If the universe were merely the accidental by-product of the big bang, then why should it obey orderly principles—or any principles at all for that matter?

Such laws are consistent with biblical creation. Natural laws exist because the universe has a Creator, God, who is logical and has imposed order on His universe (Genesis 1:1 NIV). Everything in the universe—every plant, animal, every rock, and particle of matter or light wave—is bound by laws that it has no choice but to obey.

The Bible tells us that there are laws of nature "ordinances of heaven and earth." God's logic is built into the universe, and the universe is not haphazard or arbitrary. It obeys the laws of chemistry, which are logically derived from the laws of physics, many of which can be logically derived from other laws of physics or laws of mathematics. The most fundamental laws of nature exist only because God wills them to. They are logical, and orderly in the way the Lord upholds and sustains the universe he has created. Let's examine in Genesis when God tells Noah to take of each animal but then it shows that each animal came to Noah. Noah only had to "take them" and the animals obeyed God and "showed up" to Noah. Genesis 7:1-9 NIV ¹The LORD then said to Noah, "Go into the ark, you and your whole family, because I have found you righteous in this generation. ²Take with you seven pairs of every kind of clean animal, a male and its mate, and one pair of every kind of unclean animal, a male and its mate, ³and also seven pairs of every kind of bird, male and female, to keep their various kinds alive throughout the earth. ⁴Seven days from now I will send rain on the earth for forty days and forty nights, and I will wipe from the face of the earth every living creature I have made." ⁵And Noah did all that the LORD commanded him. ⁶Noah was six hundred years old when the floodwaters came on the earth. ⁷And Noah and his sons and his wife and his sons' wives entered the ark to escape the waters of the flood. ⁸Pairs of clean and unclean animals, of birds and of all creatures that move along the ground, ⁹male and female, came to Noah and entered the ark, as God had commanded Noah. Later we see where the word of God says that he shut Noah in the ark. Genesis 7:16 ¹⁶The animals going in were male and female of every living thing, as God had commanded Noah. Then the LORD shut him in. I have always thought that Noah was safe inside the Ark because he built it according to God's specifications. I thought that perhaps it was the strength of the gopher wood and the soundness of the architecture that ensured that the waters of the flood would not come into the ark. Don't miss this.... even after Noah had built the Ark, it was God Himself who shut him in, in order to shut out the waters of the flood... In other translations this verse says "The Lord sealed them inside." May God seal us all inside his ark of protection. It is not the fact that you have locked your house that keeps you safe at night, It Is not your good driving skills that keeps you safe on the road, neither it's your healthy eating habits that keeps you healthy - only God can shut you in and shut out the devil that is seeking to devour you by convincing you to participate in the confusion in this world due to perceptions, propaganda, and narratives. What we can learn from Noah, is if we obey God will shut us in. The atheist is unable to account for the logical, orderly state of the universe. Why should the universe obey laws if there is no lawgiver? The laws of nature are perfectly consistent with biblical creation. In fact, the Bible is the foundation of natural laws.

Family relationships are significant. Your family can provide you with companionship and happiness, help you learn correct principles in a loving atmosphere, and help you prepare for eternal life. Healthy families require effort. Your family will be blessed as you do your part to strengthen it. Be cheerful, helpful, and considerate of family members.

Archbishop Michael Jackson addressed the World Meeting of Families:

> The family has always been a focus of change as well as
> being a focus of continuity. This is its double strength.
> Some families are conservative, and some families are
> radical. All of us who live in families are amateurs at
> constructing and enhancing family life. For this reason,
> forbearance and forgiveness are to be to the fore. In the
> cruel and complex globalized world in which we live, one
> in which the human person is commodified by advertising
> or by trafficking, by the quest for celebrity status or by the
> exploitation of corruption and injustice, my prayer would
> be that first and last, last and first, the family be a crucible
> of safety across generations and continents.

I pray that having that realization tempers the rage and softens the hearts of our country. While we cannot look through another's lens, we can listen as they describe what they see. We can practice empathy. We can put away pride in favor of service. We can do better. Let us venture outside of the family, comfort zones, and current social networks to grow relationships.

What can we do with us on the same page? We have to make us an action word or a peaceful transition into action, which is "we." This doesn't mean we have to agree with each other entirely, but there is a common area of agreement. How can we all be successful, grow, and benefit? Is there an opportunity to trust that we can yield to each other for the sake of united growth or benefit?

Relationships are powerful, and we must encourage an interest in others. The relationship we want to consider here is between each other as Americans. I challenge you to learn something about someone who is not the same as you. Make a list of ten individuals you believe you do not have much in common with. This could be at work, in church, in your neighborhood, or at a youth sporting event. Ask this person out to lunch, coffee, or dinner. Get to know them—without judgment.

I recommend choosing someone with different political views or religious beliefs–or even a different race. You will be surprised at what this nurturing or developing of a friendship with someone not like you will do for your processor when watching the news and listening to the propaganda that is plaguing America. I eat lunch with friends and coworkers who are Trump supporters, and I get a chance to learn their concerns about America and listen without judgment or intervention.

I find myself watching the news on CNN or Fox with a different perspective of sight and hearing. We can grow immensely from this exercise. We will begin to understand that our reactions to so much were mostly due to ignorance and not of sound knowledge or intelligence.

In the United States, the peace sign used to be a hand signal of liberty and peace. I want to encourage change. If we consider the word "We" it describes a connection and a relationship. We the People. I want us to cross our fingers to represent us as a compromise or "Co-promise" to get to know someone else who is not like you. Grow a relationship with someone who is different from you.

America is at war politically, and the strategy is no longer guerrilla warfare. The strategy today is political propaganda through social media platforms and driving fears for support and votes. In the art of war, we cannot yield to the opposing side—not even for the people—if we wish to be disciplined enough to win. If we are to heal as a nation, then relationships are key. God intended for us to love one another. When we return to trusting each other, we will be given his blessings in healing.

Love thy neighbor. This word neighbor means "stranger" and not the person next door who you can relate to. In most cases, you have so much in common with the person next door. The person you do not know is in need. That is your neighbor. That is the stranger. Again, In the parable of the Good Samaritan, the victim was a stranger. We must be willing to love the stranger. God says by doing so, we might have fed angels without even knowing it. Let us grow on what we know. The stranger is important. The stranger is the neighbor:

> Hearing that Jesus had silenced the Sadducees, the Pharisees got together. One of them, an expert in the law, tested him with this question: "Teacher, which is the greatest commandment in the Law?" Jesus replied: "'Love the Lord your God with all your heart and with

all your soul and with all your mind.' This is the first and greatest commandment. And the second is like it: 'Love your neighbor as yourself.' All the Law and the Prophets hang on these two commandments." (Matthew 22:34–40 NIV)

Jesus says all the law hangs on this. Imagine that loving a stranger (neighbor) is in the top two priorities of Christ and God. Wouldn't this world be a better place if that were our law today? The parable of the Good Samaritan was told by Jesus in the Gospel of Luke. Luke 10:25-37 NIV

The Parable of the Good Samaritan

[25] On one occasion an expert in the law stood up to test Jesus. "Teacher," he asked, "what must I do to inherit eternal life?"

[26] "What is written in the Law?" he replied. "How do you read it?"

[27] He answered, "'Love the Lord your God with all your heart and with all your soul and with all your strength and with all your mind'; and, 'Love your neighbor as yourself.'

[28] "You have answered correctly," Jesus replied. "Do this and you will live."

[29] But he wanted to justify himself, so he asked Jesus, "And who is my neighbor?"

[30] In reply Jesus said: "A man was going down from Jerusalem to Jericho, when he was attacked by robbers. They stripped him of his clothes, beat him and went away, leaving him half dead. [31] A priest happened to be going down the same road, and when he saw the man, he passed by on the other side. [32] So too, a Levite, when he came to the place and saw him, passed by on the other side. [33] But a Samaritan, as he traveled, came where the man was; and when he saw him, he took pity on him. [34] He went to him and bandaged his wounds, pouring on oil and wine. Then he put the man on his own donkey, brought him to an inn and took care of him. [35] The next day he took out two denari[j] and gave them to the innkeeper. 'Look after him,' he said, 'and when I return, I will reimburse you for any extra expense you may have.'

[36] "Which of these three do you think was a neighbor to the man who fell into the hands of robbers?"

[37] The expert in the law replied, "The one who had mercy on him."

Jesus told him, "Go and do likewise." The Good Samaritan is a first responder in the bible. The others were people with political vanity titles. Love thy neighbor.

EIGHT

Emotional
Maturity

Second in our journey through the solutions that could heal America is an area of personal growth. Do you recall the story in the preface of the book? Read it again. Growth is important. America today suffers from a few negative triggers.

"First Responders" must begin to be "Emotionally Mature".

We have often heard of the "Participation Trophy Generation" or the "Entitlement Generation". Are these just clever thoughts or real challenges with the posture today? "Emotional Maturity" is a stress factor for Americans today in that we have lost some self-control over our emotions. Many in Generation X, Y, and Z have grown up in a culture of evolution that everyone gets something for just showing up. I am here America, so where is my piece of the pie? For a Baby Boomer or Gen X, they would possibly respond with "You gotta earn it". Baby Boomers are not built to sympathize with those that have not, unless in many cases they are guided by the spirit. We must take it upon ourselves to examine our emotions in times of despair and evaluate what starts to happen in our own minds. Is my temperature elevated? Do I begin to feel threatened? Do we have a sense of vindication, revenge, or a strong desire to be justified and be heard? All these feelings are natural, but they must be controlled as well, especially in these current times. Since many today face the same emotional maturity challenges, then one triggers another and then you can witness the tit for tat going on with CNN, Fox, Democrat, Republican, Local Authority, Public, etc. You see this mindset has become contagious. Baby Boomers have joined in as a natural human defense response. Emotional Maturity is key in healing in America. It is the power within. How you respond, if you respond, and should respond begin to combat many of the political stressors in our lives. The president has significant power in his position. He heads the most powerful country in the world. Twitter, Facebook, and Social Media platforms is his real power. So much so that it aided him in becoming President of the United States. Ambitious drive and determination also contributed. I believe we should respect and honor the President, by biblical standards. I can also respect his will to achieve. I will also reveal a small key point of science to the reader as no disrespect to the President. Take away the response from any "Fire Starter" or "Flame Fanner", and you take away the power. This is for any political party. I will say this again. Take away the response, and you take away the power. We must begin to grow in our own personal Emotional Maturity as a country. Everything that is a stress, contention, or negative trigger today, consider is it because I am struggling with how I will respond? I believe we will be surprised in that moment and finally realize what the true root of the thorns in our sides are.

I attended a funeral in 2018 for a childhood friend's mom. Her brother shared a story about his mom to encourage the family. He said when he was in college at Trinity University, he somehow befriended a few gays and lesbians. He said that he grew up in a strong Catholic household that worshiped every Sunday and agreed more with traditional marriages. I will call him Carlos to protect the innocent.

Carlos shared his friends' dynamics with his mom. Mom cautioned him about his relationship with his friends and didn't want their decisions to influence his future decisions. Carlos told his mom that times were changing, and being gay or lesbian was more accepted by society now. "People are growing and not judging these situations any longer."

Carlos's mom was not convinced.

Carlos invited his friends to come home and hang out in Houston with his family for the week. He said when he got home, his mom opened the door, kissed, and hugged each of his friends. She prepared meals for them like any other friend he had ever had. By the end of the week, his mom had enjoyed so many conversations with his friends and showed them so much love. He said at the funeral that his mom didn't know how to be indifferent to anyone and that she only knew how to love.

That was such a powerful thought and moment at the funeral. Even though his mother did not agree with his friends' way of life, she could only love, and he said that she taught him that weekend that love was more significant than anything. I knew Carlos's mom, and he was right. That is what drew me to show up to the funeral. It was to support my childhood friend, his sister, but it was also because his mom loved me so much.

When I got my first promotion with AT&T, his mom cooked me dinner and baked me a cake. She even invited me over to celebrate with her family. At the time, I had a mom and dad who loved me very much, but they did not offer to celebrate my promotion. They just said, "Good job." Imagine only knowing how to love? Even in the face of differences or disagreements, if you only knew one response, love, how excellent is that in progressing experiences with people? I learned much from Carlos's submission at his mom's funeral and thought about what I could learn from it. One area that is a definite solution is to love more in this climate of emotional unrest in the United States. How can we all be like Carlos's mom and only know how to love—even when we disagree on a culture, a way of life, or political views?

In the Bible, we learned that love is the greatest of all talents we can have. In the case we just examined, love allowed someone to overcome their feelings toward a specific topic and treat people with kindness. I have been reading *Emotional Intelligence 2.0*, which coaches individuals in the areas of self-control and mind over matter. It helps with responses to adversity, conflict, and confrontation.

Emotional Intelligence 2.0 succinctly explains how to deal with emotions creatively and beneficially employ our intelligence. In this chapter, we want to approach the same thing. Political temperatures are wrapped around emotions, and in many cases, rational and logical thought are no longer relevant.

Who's right begins to conquer and smother what's right. A victory in this nature is still a loss because we didn't gain a soul, a partner, or a teammate. We simply earned a personal trophy. The result in political hostility is to understand and not shame. There is a victory in peace, and sometimes that peace comes from silence and listening. It's okay not to agree. The silence can prick the heart of another individual. You can say, "I understand."

In many cases, we understand, but we do not agree. To not agree is okay, but the opposition does not always have to know that. People have a passion for being heard. One very emotionally intelligent response was that of Randall Stephenson, the CEO of AT&T. Being emotionally intelligent does not mean you do not have any emotions, but you have control over those emotions and respond under control. Anger, sadness, and frustration can all be present, but showing too much of them harms the message. Randall Stephenson told employees how he responded to a very emotional question about unarmed Blacks getting killed by law enforcement.

Many believe that tolerance and inaction keep prejudice and resentment alive behind a mask of false civility. Communities are being stressed by racial tension, and sometimes the more rational individuals are too polite to talk about it. Recounting the experience of one of his closest friends, Randall Stephenson described how the effects of race are often hidden to those who do not have to be challenged with it daily. This is a form of privilege or an example of it outside of financial status.

Randall Stephenson admitted he had always been somewhat "confused" by his friend's racial views. His friend was a Black physician who had served three tours in Iraq and Afghanistan, but when he saw him address a mostly White church congregation about being refused service at a restaurants, it really started to open Randall's eyes to the challenges his friend was facing—even though he was educated, successful, and had served his country. These things do not remove these challenges.

The CEO's friend described being called "boy" and even fearing being stopped by police in his neighborhood. This transparency helped Randall understand the depth of his friend's frustrations. This did not mean he was seeking victimization or pity; he was just expressing a reality that he personally has lived in.

The CEO said that he started to understand his friend's anger when somebody responded to the Black Lives protest by saying, "All lives matter." When one parent says, "I love my son" in front of another parent, you don't say, "What about our daughter?" When we walk, run, or bike for MS research and funding, we don't say, "What about breast cancer?" When the president of the United States says, "God bless America," we don't say, "Shouldn't God bless all countries?" We accept each item or statement relative to its unique moment.

When a person is struggling with what's been broadcast on our airwaves and says, "Black lives matter," we should not say, "All lives matter." This response seems to justify ignoring the real need for change or even concern. The CEO was stunned to hear about his friend's experience and was no longer going to be a bystander.

There is a sin of omission in staying silent with events we know are sinful or harmful to our neighbors, friends, and families. God would expect us to speak up. This means publicly speaking up. There is a peer pressure involved with speaking up against anything that can be perceived as a notion against law enforcement. Culturally, this can be frowned upon, but who is watching our hearts? Is it God or our social arenas?

Randall Stephenson is not so much a proponent of the Black Lives Matter movement as much as he is a proponent of listening to and understanding what drives the pain. I am sure he agrees that "all lives matter" as well. His encouragement here is to listen and respond with something progressive toward the real issue. He also noticed that it didn't matter much that the physician was a soldier fighting for all Americans' rights.

Emotional maturity allows us to step back and listen. One of the strongest statements we can make to another person in a time of emotional unrest is "I hear you." In most cases, this will calm the situation. Emotions want to be heard. Over the years, I have witnessed that most experienced bosses have a certain talent. It is the talent of listening and responding with something comforting like "I understand" or "I hear you."

"We heard you" is becoming a familiar statement for many corporations to calm the unrest and uncertainty of departmental change for the better. When we grow and mature emotionally, we discontinue the counterpunch and replace it with compassion. Compassion gains a friend, and the counterpunch keeps an enemy.

The media has taken many situations and exploited them as political propaganda, and plenty of cases are complete head-scratchers. We must be emotionally mature about things in life and work together to see the good in each other. My coworker goes to lunch with me every Friday, and he even comes to pick me up on the days we work from home. He still listens to Fox News, and he still thinks Donald Trump is the greatest. I sometimes pay for his lunch, and he sometimes pays for my lunch. We believe we are not the only ones with this type of relationship in America. They are probably plentiful. What if the media went out to explore some of these areas within America? Could they help foster change and peace?

When our president speaks of "fake news" and how the news is a threat to Americans, can there be any truth to this? If the news is only sharing a perception of harm toward the current administration without surveying the people who do not complete online surveys on their websites, how do they know the American public's thoughts? I say this as not as a proponent of the president's claims but as transparency to the thoughts of many who do not always have a voice because they have chosen to be emotionally mature about the perceptions of this nation. They call this group of individuals the "silent majority". They tip the scale on elections and cannot be quantified in most cases. They are the group that perceptions can be changed. They are emotionally mature and have no allegiance to any party, but to the good of all. Just recently many political activist attempt to identify that they know they are out there and they try and appeal to them. Good luck. This group is a researched group of individuals that do not show their hands.

CNN and Fox News should collaborate on stories to create harmony among people with different political views and other cultures to help inspire Americans to try to find peace among ourselves. In many cases, this is already happening, but the media is not covering it. That approach is harming our society and begs the question of whether what we see daily is just fake news because it does not always represent the "Silent Majority".

The Silent Majority are the largest part of a country's population that consists of people who are not actively involved in politics and do not express their political opinions publicly.

To have emotional maturity is to have specific control over one's emotions. An emotionally mature person has experienced the spectrum of emotions, understands the consequences of each, and knows the benefits of being in control of them. Most importantly, an emotionally mature person knows what kinds of things set off different emotions in them, and they know how to identify their emotions. They don't panic and try to determine what they feel and how they should react.

A potato that is placed in boiling water will eventually soften up to the point where you can grab a fork and mash it easily. When an egg is placed in boiling water, it will become hard within five or ten minutes. A coffee bean dissolves in boiling water and affects the water around it. It changes the water's color, the aroma of the water, and you no longer even see the coffee bean because it has become part of the water. Our emotions should be more like the coffee bean and not like the potato or the egg. Do not let the environment around us affect our state of being. Let our positive state affect the environment around us and draw others to want to consume the pleasant aroma and peaceful bliss.

As we try to grow and mature emotionally, we can learn about a few areas of awareness:

- emotional responsibility
- emotional honesty
- emotional openness
- emotional assertiveness
- emotional understanding
- emotional detachment

When we become emotionally responsible, a person reaches level one of emotional maturity. They realize that they can no longer view their emotional state as the responsibility of external forces such as people, places, things, forces, fate, and spirits. They learn to drop expressions from their speech that disown their feelings or show a helpless or victim attitude toward their feelings. Expressions such as "They made me feel," "It made me feel," and "I made them feel" denote external emotional responsibility. They should be changed into "I statements."

"You make me so mad when you do that" becomes "I feel mad when you do that because …"

Being honest with our emotions concerns the willingness of a person to know and own their feelings. This is a necessary step for self-acceptance and self-understanding. The issue of resistance to self-discovery is dealt with at this level. Resistance issues stem from a person's conscious and unconscious fears of dealing directly with the critical voices they hear inside their minds.

When people don't learn emotional coping skills, they generally lose most interactions with their internal adversaries, internal critics, negative self-talk, and hyperactive conscience. Therefore, people's fears of emotional honesty are based on past ego pain from being internally judged as worse than, lower than, or inferior to others.

People at this level of emotional honesty know how to choose to feel so that they can keep from being hurt. They also know how to choose not to interact with their inner accusers by ignoring, distracting, or redirecting techniques. "To thine own self be true" is the primary goal at this level of maturity.

We begin to grow into an emotional openness with ourselves and others by sharing feelings in an appropriate manner and at the right times. Persons at this level experience and learn the value of letting go of emotions and the dangers involved in hiding feelings from the self and others.

Self-disclosure is a critical issue at this level of emotional maturity, but it will never be as important as the willingness to be open to experiencing feelings as they arise without critical voices trying to change, control, or condemn those feelings. The dangers of suppressing feelings and the value inherent in exploring feelings and allowing them internal expression are investigated over time.

Emotional maturity comes with the accountability of emotions and their impact on others. A person at this level of work enters a new era of joyful self-expression. The primary goal is to be able to ask for and receive the nurturing they need and want first from the self and then from others. They assert their emotional needs in all their relationships if it is safe to do so. As a secondary goal, they learn how to express feelings appropriately, including how to convey an emotion without aggressive or manipulative overtones.

A person at this level of emotional maturity makes time for feelings—and respects those feelings. They understand the connections between suppressed feelings, harmful stress, and illness. We are closer to emotional graduation when we consider unity with opposites. We possess emotional maturity and understand the actual cause-and-effect processes of personal responsibility and emotional irresponsibility.

Self-concepts are understood to be the problem that interferes with emotional responsibility. This person realizes that it is impossible to have a good self-concept without a complementary inadequate self-concept. Because of the nature of knowledge and the formation of self-concepts, these people experience firsthand that all self-concepts contain their opposites. Knowing that one half of some self-concept duality is still active in them, even if they hide it in darkness (unconsciousness), they begin to regularly leap beyond the pitfalls of self-concept, self-image, and self-construct.

The ego plays a big role in emotional maturity, and the superego controls even more. An emotionally detached person begins to live without the burden of self-concepts, self-images, self-constructs, group concepts, and thing concepts. This person is only aware of the self as a process, as a sensing being, as an experiencing being, as a living vessel, and as unknowable and untrappable because the self is alive and not static or fixed.

This person has died to the life of self as self-concepts. True detachment from all self-concepts has occurred. Thus, actual separation from others has also happened, which means that absolute emotional responsibility has been achieved or discovered. Without self-concepts to defend or promote, this person can remain unaffected by the blame game. Without self-concepts to protect or enable, this person can experience unconditional love for their enemies. This moment allows us to be kind to each other regardless of our opposing views.

We can deliver kindness and love unto others without conditions. Emotional maturity is an excellent platform of wisdom for all people. Let us always do a litmus test when we are about to share our feelings on any topic. There are three questions we should ask ourselves before we react, respond, or speak on a subject. Is this my perception, based on my culture and upbringing? Is this strategy based on a political agenda? Have I done enough research?

When watching CNN, Fox News, or any of the major broadcast news channels, spend time asking yourself these questions as you watch the news. Do I feel a certain way based on culture? Do I feel this way due to a political strategy? Have I investigated it? If the answer to any of these is a yes or no, solve that answer first to respond with a higher, more reliable communication style. With great power, comes great responsibility.

Let us agree with this as one team in America:

> Like newborn babies, crave pure spiritual milk, so that by it you may grow up in your salvation. (1 Peter 2:2 NIV)

God gives everything purpose and—in time—understanding. Biblical history has patterns, and in those patterns, many of God's prophets and even Christ had to be protected by being sent to a foreign land. Moses was sent to Egypt to save him from being killed. Christ was sent to Bethlehem to save the child from being killed. I can only believe that a few great individuals are presently being detained or preserved for a great plan one day by God himself. What one means for harm, God will mean for good—and unfortunate becomes fortunate by God's plan:

> When a foreigner resides among you in your land, do not mistreat them. The foreigner residing among you must be treated as your native-born. Love them as yourself, for you were foreigners in Egypt. I am the Lord your God. (Leviticus 19:33–34 NIV)

Many did not know what Moses or Christ were going to become even though they showed care and grace for them in their infancy. The king ordered the killing of the children, but they survived in a foreign land:

> Do not forget to show hospitality to strangers, for by so doing some people have shown hospitality to angels without knowing it. (Hebrews 13:2 NIV)

A child in the womb does not have a greater value than a child in the room. Let your zeal and care be for both. We cannot let political parties supersede our faith. God will judge us. We cannot allow peer pressure and cultural identification to conquer our Christian posture. There should be no lampshades on our lights. Speak life, defend life, speak love, and defend love. Jesus instructed us that all laws rest on this:

> One of them, an expert in the law, tested him with this question: "Teacher, which is the greatest commandment in the Law?" Jesus replied: "'Love the Lord your God with all your heart and with all your soul and with all your mind.' This is the first and greatest commandment. And the second is like it: 'Love your neighbor as yourself.' All the Law and the Prophets hang on these two commandments." (Matthew 22:35–40 NIV)

NINE

NOT OFFENDED

The third solution in Healing America is the choice we all can make to not be offended. This is one of the most powerful decision we can make today. If we want to be a "First Responder" and remember that means to not respond, then we must invoke the choice to "*Not Be Offended*".

"Frist Responders are rarely Offended."

Imagine for a sec, everyone in American going on a 72 hour fast of not being offended? What do you think would happen? Extreme peace? It may seem Elementary in thought and that it cannot be this simple at times, but just the reduction of what we take offense to will greatly improve our quality of life today. We can choose to not be offended. We can advance relationships because of this choice and reduce waisted breaths responding to things that are offensive. Remember our friend Jammer in Chapter 1? He was offended and he begin to be encouraged to be more offended. The fire was started and then the flame was being fanned for Jammer. The current climate in America is all about being offended, and to be offended more and more. Political strategies drive at this, because they have detected the emotional immaturity of their audiences, and so they use this to their advantage. Imagine that you have engaged in the re-post, re-post, of the Flame Fanning because of one's own Emotional Immaturity?

"One who is offended, will in return Offend."

Have you ever heard that hurt people will then hurt people? It drives the people daily and takes away a significant portion of the American Public's quality of life. This strategy robs Americans of a peaceful spirit each day. We must take a strong stance on not being offended. Ignore the offenders. Do not respond. Become a "First Responder".

Understanding in those moments of offense, begin to ask yourself a few questions, rhetorically.

- Is it real?
- Is it political strategy?
- Is it my perception?
- Is it vindication?

Jammer in Chapter 1 realized that he being offended was about to lead him to do something he was going to regret later and possibly would have impeded his advancement within the company in later times. Choose *"Not to be Offended"*. Keep your power. Control your emotions (become emotional intelligent). Grow and be stronger. The result from these steps will increase your quality of life and healthy mindset as we start healing. One can be a "Hero" in their own story, by drawing strength from these areas we have presented to *"Not to be Offended"*. Expand your relationships outside of your comfort zone, improve on your emotional maturity, and choose *"Not to be Offended"*. In those moments, just say it to yourself. I am going to choose not to be offended, keep my power, keep my peace, and move on. First Responders do this regularly.

In 1997, I graduated from college with a degree in Criminal Justice Law Enforcement: Police Science. Believe it or not, I know a little about some of the current events with police excessive use of force and the science that is behind those behavioral patterns.

My first out of college job in 1998 was not in my field. I was working on going into the Houston Police Department, but I chose instead to apply at Union Pacific Railroad because it paid more money starting out. On my first day on the job, I reported to Rosenberg, Texas, and I met the team I would be working with at an office converted from an old railroad cart.

When I walked into the office the first day, a little early, I met my Boss, who was at least sixty years old. He was a retired marine who we called Bernie. After each member showed up that morning, and we introduced ourselves. Bernie open the meeting up by saying, "This is a man's job here, and we are all men here. Sometimes I use offensive, derogatory language on the job, and if you have a problem with that, you may be working at the wrong place."

In the room, there were three Caucasian males who some would call "rednecks." There was an African American who some would call a "brother." There were two Latinos, and I'm not sure what some would call them.

Bernie was a German with a military background. He is an old-school leader, but he was very good. I used the words derogatory language to replace the word Bernie actually used to describe the African Americans he would come across during work hours or even those who worked for him. The word is too inappropriate to write. I believe you know the word.

After Bernie made that statement, I looked at the other African American who had been working on the team to see if he was going to respond. He did not.

I took it upon myself to respond.

> Me: Bernie, I would appreciate if you would not use that language around me.

> Bernie: Well, you can't work around us with a chip on your shoulder.

> Me: "I am asking you to please not use that language at work around me, sir.

Later, we drove out to Flatonia, Texas, which is the halfway point between Houston and San Antonio. We had a project to install centralized track circuits so that the trains could see the signals for the right way to proceed down the track. Electric switches were put in to eliminate the train from having to stop for a brakeman or switchman to have to get off the train to throw a switch.

Our project was going to speed train traffic by three times the amount and result in more revenue for Union Pacific. This new technology would eliminate the need for someone to get off the train to throw a switch, and there would be no need for that job title any longer.

When we began to work in Flatonia, Bernie would often give me the most challenging jobs. He would often have me and two other minorities digging and burying cable close to the train track. A backhoe could do the work, but due to my words of contention, I was on his bad list. I worked hard to try to prove that I was the best worker on the team and would take on each day's hard work with a great attitude.

I was determined to prove to Bernie that African Americans were not at all like the stereotypes he was probably familiar with. By the ninetieth day on the job, I could tell that Bernie was impressed with me. Knowing that I was being accepted for at least being a hard worker helped me to sleep at night.

In one month in Flatonia, we had eleven straight days of hundred-plus-degree weather. By the end of the week, we had lost most of our team to heat exhaustion except a fifty-year-old man named Bruce and me. By the weekend, Bernie asked me to drive the truck out to the site, and it was just he and I left to work that weekend, due to the high temperatures and the loss of most of our team's stamina. I thought, *Should I be afraid of what Bernie may have me doing today and play sick or go home? Should I just see what he has in store?*

That morning, Bernie told me to stop the truck and said, "Blount, you are all right with me. You have done well. Don't let anyone tell you any different. You are my guy." He patted my chest and told me we were going to take it easy today since we were the only ones on the clock. He even told me he would pay for twenty-four hours of work for two days, even though were going to take it easy for the weekend.

We can decide not to be offended. We can also decide to challenge perceptions and stereotypes. We can decide to make these traditional notions a falsehood. Many will say Bernie was a racist. Maybe he was. Maybe he never encountered anything different than what he had been exposed to his entire life. We can approach these situations with character and determination to help people grow. It is on us many times to decide to love in such a way. Agape is love in spite of or a sacrificial love that is not conditional on how I am treated or if it will be reciprocated. Bernie and I became good coworkers, a team.

The success I had with Bernie was that I chose not to be offended. It was huge. I was determined to erase any stereotypes he had of African Americans. I didn't want to lose my cool and be the next angry Black man he encountered—even though I probably would have been justified. I was after a relationship with Bernie. I was twenty-three years old, but I knew I could win him over.

I bought my first home while working for Union Pacific, and after three years, I moved on to a corporate position at AT&T. Another boss once told me a story that helped him in his corporate growth. This story was about "choosing to be offended." This is a potential hot topic, but I think it is important for our careers, our companies, and our families. John Schroff was a long-term AT&T employee. He started in IT in New Jersey and made his way down to Dallas and then Houston in the network sales organization.

John would tell me stories from time to time about how he was raised, including how his Pakistani father kidnapped him and his brother from his Polynesian mother when he was very young. John is an interesting fellow, and I still keep in contact with him. He retired from the company a few years back. When we got into arguments with AT&T operations folks or our customers, he would say, "Jim, you are choosing to be offended." Given the world we live in with social media defining the norms for our society and the 24-7 news cycle, we are often told by everyone how we should act and what should and should not offend us. As a global company, we come from very different cultures with our own biases and cultural norms.

How much do my biases and social norms affect my interactions? Did I take offense when I should not have taken offense? On the other side of the coin, given how much of our communication today is via email and other nonverbal and nonvisual communication, did I say something in the email I would not have said face-to-face? If so, should I have waited to send that email? Did I unintentionally insult or offend someone? If I did, what should I do?

Here is another story about a day in Texas when it snowed, which is rare for Texas, but people like to go outside and play in the snow no matter what their age is. It Snowed once in Houston, and here is how the day went:

8:00.   I made a snowman.

8:10.   A feminist passed by and asked why I didn't make a snow woman.

8:15.   So, I made a snow woman.

8:17.   My feminist neighbor complained about the snow woman's voluptuous chest, saying it objectified snow women everywhere.

8:20.   The gay couple living nearby threw a hissy fit and moaned that it could have been two snowmen instead.

8:22.   The transgender person asked why I didn't just make one snow person with detachable parts.

8:25.   The vegans at the end of the lane complained about the carrot nose since veggies are food and not for decorating snow figures.

8:28.   I was called a racist because the snow couple was White.

8:30.   I used food coloring to make one of the snow couple a different color and be more racially inclusive.

8:37.   I was accused of using blackface on the "snow persons."

8:39.   The Middle Eastern gentleman across the road demanded the snow woman be covered up.

8:40.   The police arrived because someone had been offended.

8:42.   The feminist neighbor complained again that the broomstick of the snow woman needed to be removed because it depicted women in a domestic role.

8:43.   The council equality officer arrived and threatened me with eviction.

8:45.   A TV news crew from ABC showed up. I was asked if I know the difference between snowmen and snow women? I replied, "Snowballs," and I am now called sexist.

9:00.   I was on the news as a suspected terrorist, racist, homophobe, and sensibility offender, bent on stirring up trouble during difficult weather.

9:10.   I was asked if I had any accomplices. My children were taken by social services.

9:29.   Far-left protesters were offended by everything and marched down the street, demanding for me to be arrested.

9:45.   The boss called and fired me because of the negative association with work that had been all over social media.

10:00.   I cry into my drink because all I wanted to do was build a snowman.

Of course, this did not really happen, but I think we can all agree on how things can get out of hand when trying to please everyone and not offend so many different views. I'm sorry about the snowman and wish I had not been so fascinated with snow. This is a hypothetical story, but I believe many people might read this and think it could really happen.

Taking offense seems to be an obligation or a natural response to someone else. When we see things that we do not like, we feel like we have no choice but to become upset and express it adamantly. We may view our responses as outside of our hands. We are only reacting to others. Like most things, however, taking offense is really an issue with the self. It has nothing to do with the person who is offending you and everything to do with you. Yes, some people say and do things that may seem ridiculous to you, but have you ever thought about how you say and do things that are ridiculous to others? The issue of being offended has to do with how we choose to respond.

In the same way that we choose to be offended, we can also choose not to be offended, which has several advantages:

- We can listen to and understand others better.
- We increase our opportunities to learn.
- We can more easily resolve conflict.
- We grow our ability to influence the world around us.

Once you choose to be offended, your ability to make a difference will be negated, but if you decide not to be offended, you have taken the first step toward influence. Making this choice, however, is difficult. Here are five ways to help you change how you respond.

Try to find value in every person. You have to believe that every person in the world has intrinsic value and then look for it. Understand that their perspective is unique to them, and that is beneficial. Seek what is helpful instead of being focused on what you find offensive.

Always be asking what they can teach you. Search for what you can learn. You will be amazed at what you will find. Listening today is a lost art, and many people listen anxiously, waiting to respond. Practice sincere listening skills daily. Learn to listen. Most of us don't. We listen to people we agree with because we already like what they are saying, but we rarely listen to anyone else.

The only way to understand another person is to hear what they have to say. Listen with the goal of understanding—not arguing. If someone is offending you, it is an excellent time to stop talking and start listening. If nothing else, you are less likely to say something you will regret. Try something new. Like strange food, the reason we don't like something different is because we haven't tried it.

Ignorance leads to fear. Fear leads to being offended. Start with something simple like food or a cultural experience. If you feel courageous enough, switch to CNN or Fox News, depending on your political persuasion. Develop a spirit of courage and adventure. The only way to understand a different perspective is to try it. Apologize. One of the main reasons we are so easily offended is pride. Pride is one of the seven deadly sins and is behind all evil in some fashion or another.

The most humbling thing you can do is apologize when you are wrong. We are all wrong at some point. When it is your turn, do something beneficial about it. Apologize. It will force you to be humble, and it will speak volumes to the other person. Today, find someone you have offended and apologize to them. Be a friend. Don't feel like it is your obligation to change people. Being a friend is about loving them where they are. Friends encourage and help others. They find what a person needs and then help them meet those needs with no strings attached.

The people who are in the best position to influence us are faithful friends. Being offended is really a selfish way to treat people. The response is focused on ourselves and not on the other person. It is about what we want them to be. It is about our desire to change them. The only person in this world that you can change is you.

The only way to remove offense from your life is to choose to respond differently. Are you easily offended? What have you found that helps you choose otherwise? Start working on it today. Let us grow through what we know. Whether it's self-inflicted or deliberate, we've all been offended to some degree or another: a car cuts us off, causing a near-fatal accident, a rude store clerk embarrasses you, a friend betrays your trust, or a relative mindlessly insults or criticizes you. I do not mean to minimize the pain of those who have been physically or mentally abused. While all these burdens are horrific and unimaginable, they do not mean anyone is sentenced to a life of bitterness and revenge. Those feelings of anger, frustration, resentment, and pain can poison our attitudes, outlooks, and hope. The idea of not taking offense, forgiving, and giving second chances destroys our victim mentality. If we remain the victim, we feel entitled to snap at the clumsy waiter, be impatient with the person in front of you, and criticize anyone who tries to help. The story you're replaying right now may have been the worst thing anyone can imagine, but do you allow what happened to control how you feel?

Maybe we let those feelings simmer and stew and poison us from the inside out. Maybe we obsess about the offense over and over like a moth circling a light. However we react, the choice is always ours. This life is too short to be lived nursing animosity or documenting wrongs of those closest to us. To be offended is a choice we make; it is not a condition inflicted or imposed upon us.

There is real strength and freedom in rising above our emotions and not being offended. Imagine that power for a moment. Once we decide to not be offended, we have a victory. We are led to believe that we should be offended sometimes and think we deserve revenge, justice, or vindication. Which voice are we going to allow to continue to poison our emotional, physical, and spiritual self?

Stopping the vicious cycle is hard, but I've found seven ideas to replace your resentment with healthier and happier thought processes. As with any new habit, there is intentional effort involved. I strongly believe this effort and discipline leads to a mentally healthier way of living. Consider these five approaches to something that is offensive to us.

1. Don't Take Offense

"Take" is defined as a voluntary action to grab, hold, or grip something. It goes back to choice. We can decide not to take offense. Let the opportunity to grab those feelings pass you by. What someone does or says to you is what Brooke Castillo calls your "circumstance." What we decide to think and feel about what the other person did is our choice and will ultimately affect the way we respond.

2. The Law of the Garbage Truck

David Polly discovered this concept. It's an "It's them, not me" way of thinking. He teaches how some people are like garbage trucks. They run around full of garbage, frustration, anger, and disappointment until they need somewhere to dump it. Sometimes, it might be right on you. We may not have a choice about whether we are at the receiving end of these dump trucks, but we do have a choice in how we react. We can choose to smile, wave, and then move on.

3. Don't Let Pride Cloud Your Perspective

Our natural tendency is to believe our assumptions and ways of thinking are correct, but don't allow your pride to burn bridges just because someone points out an imperfection. Sometimes we are the problem. The delivery may be a little off, but what a friend is saying might be right on track. This kind of honesty can hurt the most because it is coming from someone we love. Listen to what they are saying and then chalk it up to constructive criticism. Let your love for the person overshadow your pride.

4. The Golden Rule

What about the times you offend someone? Just like the Golden Rule, we can react to others in the same way we would like to be treated. I feel grateful when someone graciously lets go of my offhand comment or thoughtless remark and chooses to treat me kindly. Having experienced both sides of an offense, wouldn't you rather be the one who reacts in a gracious, more gentle way?

5. Don't Let Others Define You

Seeking approval or acceptance from others is a weak foundation for building self-worth. When we compare ourselves to others, we are putting our weaknesses up against their strengths. Our self-worth should not depend on what someone else thinks or says.

God has ordained work as a stewardship of his created world (Genesis 1:28; 2:15 NIV). He has designed work for his glory and our good. How might we glorify God at work?

Playing professional sports is a job or a career. This is how many people provide for their families. We must believe that all legitimate work is holy or unholy before God based on our faith and not on the nature of the work itself:

But whoever has doubts is condemned if he eats because the eating is not from faith. For whatever does not proceed from faith is sin. (Romans 14:23 NIV)

Be just and honest in all your dealings with money. A false balance is an abomination to the Lord, but a just weight is his delight. (Proverbs 11:1 NIV)

Fans and players see professional athletes' wages and careers as "earned." In the spiritual realm, it is a grace and blessing from God. What God has given can only be lost through arrogance and denial that God gave it. God tells us to use the wages earned by our work to provide for and bless others:

Anyone who does not provide for their relatives, and especially for their own household, has denied the faith and is worse than an unbeliever. (1 Timothy 5:8 NIV)

Anyone who has been stealing must steal no longer, but must work, doing something useful with their own hands, that they may have something to share with those in need. (Ephesians 4:28 NIV)

The Word of God encourages us to grow our skills, work hard, and strive for excellence:

They will serve before kings; they will not serve before officials of low rank. (Proverbs 22:29 NIV)

All hard work brings a profit, but mere talk leads only to poverty. (Proverbs 14:23 NIV).

Christians and Christian athletes should be a part of unification and not divisiveness. We should be a voice of wisdom among the turmoil in professional sports:

In the same way, let your light shine before others, that they may see your good deeds and glorify your Father in heaven. (Matthew 5:16 NIV).

Exemplify love for your neighbor in how you interact with your colleagues. Do everything in love. (1 Corinthians 16:14 NIV)

Speak the Gospel to your colleagues.

We are therefore Christ's ambassadors, as though God were making his appeal through us. We implore you on Christ's behalf: Be reconciled to God. (2 Corinthians 5:20 NIV)

Let us remember the Word of God:

Whatever you do, work at it with all your heart, as working for the Lord, not for human masters, since you know that you will receive an inheritance from the Lord as a reward. It is the Lord Christ you are serving. (Colossians 3:23–24 NIV)

Slaves, in reverent fear of God submit yourselves to your masters, not only to those who are good and considerate, but also to those who are harsh. (1 Peter 2:18 NIV)

Focus on the work you've been given:

Those who work their land will have abundant food, but those who chase fantasies will have their fill of poverty. (Proverbs 28:19 NIV)

Speaking words of grace—not edging on the revolution:

Do not let any unwholesome talk come out of your mouths, but only what is helpful for building others up according to their needs, that it may benefit those who listen. (Ephesians 4:29 NIV)

If someone apologizes, let it be good enough. Are we denying repentance or forgiveness? Imagine God telling us we didn't mean it. Let it be enough:

Obey them not only to win their favor when their eye is on you, but as slaves of Christ, doing the will of God from your heart. Serve wholeheartedly, as if you were serving the Lord, not people, because you know that the Lord will reward each one for whatever good they do, whether they are slave or free. (Ephesians 6:6–8 NIV)

Section 3 – Social Challenge

Make a video karaoke singing "Can You Feel It" by the Jackson 5. Invite friends, co-workers, teammates, or anyone in your social arena. Make it hype, fun, energetic, send a message with the music, and sing with some passion. We will set up a go-fund-me page so people (even celebrities) can contribute and, at the end of 2021, will reward someone with that money from the Go-Fund-Me donations. 50% will go to that winner, and the other 50% will go to the Charity of the Winner's Choice. An organization could win or a single person. Review the lyrics of the song and consider how they can apply to the current temperatures in America and help us to become one again. The blood that is inside of you, is inside of me. You can use YouTube or TikTok.

SECTION IV

THE BENEFIT

TEN

A Higher Quality of Life

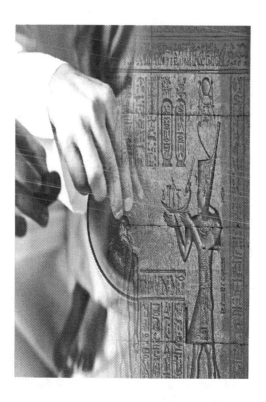

The turtle's safety zone is in its shell. It is there to protect it, but not to hinder its ability to move or to progress. Our comfort zones are there also, not to hinder our progress or keep us from growing.

In America we have been in a similar situation to the man at the pool in our opening scripture presented in our intro to the setting of this book Healing America. Sitting by the water with excuses of not getting in, to help ourselves. *"A Higher Quality of Life"* is what America offers. We all but must extend our necks to achieve it and come out of our comfort zones to capture it. Do *"We"* want to get well was the question that Christ asked the man. America *"Do "We" want to get well?* The man had so many excuses. America, we have so many excuses today. Well they did it to us and now we are doing it to them. They are hypocrites. They want our guns. They kill babies. So many stones thrown and vindication desired, that we care not to get well sometimes. We have to pick up our matt, our comfort zones, and begin to move. We have to be obedient to God's word and love our neighbor. That includes the liberal and the conservative. Get well. Heal.

Obstacles and challenges are not there to help us fail, but to help us strengthen so that we might sustain what we can achieve. We sustain through an inner endurance. The diamond does not detest pressure, because it was by pressure that its beauty was revealed. America's beauty came from a history of pressure, adversity, and darkness. Without these events, we would not be who we are today. It can be perceived we would be better without our History, without our birth defects, without our darkness, but we would not be much more than cold coal waiting for its pressures of life. In Chapters 10-12 will be about what is in it for me or the benefits to the knowledge shares we have had thus far. We have mainly focused on what we can control. I can control my perception. I can control my response. I can research further. I can choose not to be offended. I can choose to listen. I can choose to try and understand. I can choose to respect cultures even if I do not fully agree with them. I can choose to be mindful of the media's positions and biased delivery of the news. I can choose to grow. I can choose to have empathy. I can choose to not be drawn into the social media debates around topics that I am socially biased too. It is time to take back our power to decide and not discard the desire to be justified or vindicate ourselves. I can choose to keep my power and not yield it to the perceptions that someone else is shaping. I can choose not to allow the person that is shaking the jar, to include me in the chaos and confusion. When I choose a positive response, I give myself the power to have a higher quality of life. In America today we should feel some measure of desperation. We should allow that to be an inspiration to change. A person's ego can become a veil between them and God. Leadership can teach people ego and pride, or it can teach humility and silent strength. Humility becomes the precursor to healing what emotional pains we feel and even what we do not fully understand. Humility directly solicits God's support. Pride, God detest.

"Story of Pride and Ego"

In 2002, while working as an AT&T call center rep for residential services, I decided to go back to school to get my real estate license. After two years as a real estate agent, I decided to go back to school to become a real estate broker and start my own real estate company. It took me some time to get promoted at AT&T, and I didn't have the patience to wait on a promotion.

My son was born in 2001, and I felt like I needed to put myself in a better position financially since I was growing a family. When I became a real estate broker, I was doing very well. I bought a home in Sienna Plantation, a fast-growing community in Southwest Houston. I didn't let the title of the community development offend me. My home was beautiful, and I bought a Mercedes S500 AMG sedan. Much of what I had purchased probably made me look privileged, but a lot of home sales and hard work went into it.

In 2006, I was making more in real estate than at AT&T. In 2005, I received a promotion to the business call center manager and had a team of nineteen reps. I also had a real estate brokerage with twenty-seven agents. My earnings were up, and my stress was up as well. In addition to that, my son had team sports and other extracurricular activities. I thought life was going great, and I had titles that made me feel very proud.

Some grit and grind can go a long way in America. I had taken full advantage of the land of opportunity until the mortgage crisis struck in 2006. I had become a fan of George Bush as president in terms of the response to 9/11 and because of how easy it was to process loans for clients. Many people were able to purchase homes, but in many cases, they were using bogus earnings.

I was appreciative of the low taxes under George Bush. Some people survived the crisis and kept their homes, but many did not. When the mortgage crisis was in full stride, my agents started dropping monthly. After eighteen months, I was down to four agents, and my income was reduced by 70 percent. I had bought my Mercedes and home with the two incomes combined. My stress levels were up, and I had not been paying income taxes as I should have. I owed the government more than twenty-five thousand dollars in back taxes, and eventually, they garnished my AT&T paycheck. I had a levy on my home from back property taxes and so much more. I quickly went up the mountain and then back down. *The land of opportunity? What happened?* Pride and arrogance had their day with me as I was prospering. I didn't go to church as much anymore and made everything personal in my life. Pride hurt me more than anything else.

I didn't have work and spiritual balance. I was not planning for failure; I was living with a posture of invincibility. I eventually started having extreme anxiety, and I gained about thirty pounds in six months, which was not good. My anxiety was so bad that I was visiting the emergency room about twice a month.

I had an anxiety attack in a business meeting at AT&T, and it was very embarrassing. My health was beginning to fade. I was being given sleeping pills and Xanax and an assortment of antidepressants. My quality of life went from remarkable to dark in about a year. I was also diagnosed with sleep apnea and had to start sleeping with a CPAP.

I thought about filing for bankruptcy, but I just kept saying that sometimes we must let go and rebuild. I had a very close friend who was Catholic, and I mentioned that I was disappointed in myself because I only make it to church about two Sundays per month. My friend said she could not remember the last time she missed church. I belonged to the Church of Christ, and we pride ourselves on our spiritual stamina and discernment. *Why can't I make it to church every Sunday?* On that day, I decided what my New Years' resolution was going to be.

In America, we do not make significant changes until the start of the year. We try to get all the games out of our system and then decide on the change at the appropriate time. I began to go to church every Sunday for a whole year. My home had foreclosed, and I was paying back the IRS. I moved into an apartment, sold my Mercedes, and purchased a Ford F-150. Each year, I challenged myself to go further with the church. I started attending men's retreats, fellowships, and workshops. I was growing in faith with good momentum.

Story of Humility and God's Favor

I had to attend a sales kickoff meeting in Dallas for AT&T, and my parents were worried about my anxiety flaring up on the flight. Those who suffer with anxiety will understand that planes do not do us so well. When I got on the flight with five if my coworkers, I was determined to sit by one of them so that I could relax and have someone to talk to on the short forty-minute flight, but my coworkers all grabbed seats with no openings next to them.

I began to panic and realized that I was not going to be able to sit by any of them. I thought, *I should have told one of them about my issue.* I found a seat in the back and sat down. No one was on either side of me. Finally, a man with an AT&T badge sat down next to me, and I felt some relief. I did not recognize him, but we began to chat about our positions at AT&T. This co-worker seemed to be a very genuine person, gentle, and kind, and the conversation was better than what I would have experienced with my coworkers.

When we landed in Dallas, I called my parents and shared the experience on the flight. After a few days in Dallas, we headed back to

Houston. The same gentleman sat by me on the plane. I was relieved, and my anxiety was doing much better.

I continued my commitment to going to church every Sunday for more than a year. On the first Sunday back from Dallas, I was very excited as I went to church. In my heart, I felt like God had sent that gentleman to comfort me. I attended a medium-sized congregation Church of Christ in Sugarland.

My parents met me at church, and we sat down and started our usual singing of hymns. After the sermon and worship were over, I felt a tap on my shoulder. When I looked up, it was the gentleman from the plane. I introduced him to my parents, and he said he was a member of the church and was a deacon there. He usually went to the ten o'clock service, and we normally went to the seven o'clock service, and we had never run across each other before. My mom immediately got sort of teary-eyed because she connected all the dots and understood that God was looking out for me.

As we exited to the parking lot, an older woman approached me, shook my hand, and looked directly in my eyes. She said, "Baby, you've got to sleep. You must sleep and rest that mind. That mind is powerful, and it needs rest. You have to sleep." She shook my mom's hand and walked off with her son. My mom and I turned toward each other, and we both had tears in our eyes. I had not been sleeping well, but I had been trying. I was unwilling to take anxiety medicine, and I didn't want to take any sleeping pills. I was terrified of becoming addicted to them. I suffered through it, and I said I was going to rely on God.

I decided I would start using my CPAP machine at night to get better sleep. The CPAP machine was not sexy, and I was trying to be "the guy." All Ego. Eventually, I recovered financially, and I also tackled my anxiety. In 2013 I graduated from Minister School and was asked to go on a Mission Trip to Guyana and I preached there 6 days and had over 16 baptisms that week. I never looked back spiritually. To God be the Glory. After my first mission trip to Guyana, I went back to the US and never had another anxiety attack. I started dating the woman who would become my wife in the coming years. GiGi was a great fit for the life I was involved in and I was a great fit for the life she was seeking. She was what I had always prayed for. We now have a blended family and have been together for 6 years. God is everything. My life was so dark, but my life has so much light now.

Two different stories with two different outcomes. In the Bible in the Book of Philippians 3:7-8 NIV the Apostle Paul says "7 But whatever were gains to me I now consider loss for the sake of Christ. 8 What is more, I consider everything a loss because of the surpassing worth of knowing Christ Jesus my Lord, for whose sake I have lost all things. I consider them garbage, that I may gain Christ". I believe this whole-heartedly today. For me to gain Christ, I had to lose. Character is rarely revealed in a win, yet it is in a loss that we are shown our strength.

What does this have to do with quality of life? A few messages that can be drawn out from this. We live in the land of opportunity, but if we decide to live with pride, greed, and no relationship with God, we can destroy ourselves—and that will not be systemic racism or any other oppression. We can become our own oppressors by our own arrogance. When we live a life with God at the center—humble, respectful, and balance—we can be very effective in our pursuit of happiness with outstanding sustainability. This is often the difference in this life and our quality of life. Try God. He will deliver. He dug me out the darkest of times, and I have never looked back at those days. Instead, I chose to grow.

What does it mean to have a higher quality of life? Is it not one of the drivers that drove the discovery of America, religious freedom, and a higher quality of life? Notice the word "discovery." It was discovery of a culture and not so much of a country. We have repented and turned away from "found" America. We choose to be no longer offended. Americans have a desire for a higher quality of life at each demographic or economic level.

How is quality of life defined? It is an overarching term for the quality of the various domains in life. It is a standard level that consists of the expectations of an individual or society for a good experience. These expectations are guided by the values, goals, and sociocultural context in which an individual lives. It is a subjective, multidimensional concept that defines a standard level for emotional, physical, material, and social well-being. It serves as a reference against which an individual or society can measure the different domains of one's own life. The extent to which one's own life coincides with this desired standard level—or the degree to which these domains give satisfaction and contribute to one's subjective well-being—is life satisfaction.

Rules for a Higher Quality of Life

1. Maintain Healthy Relationships

Relationships play an essential role in mental health. Research shows that healthy and supportive relationships increase happiness, life satisfaction, and psychological well-being, and they can also reduce the risk of suicide. However, not all relationships are created equal. Negative associations can yield toxic situations that involve conflict and stress. Disconnecting from unhealthy relationships and fostering healthy ones is vital to your well-being.

2. Get a Good Night's Sleep

Whether you're staying up late because of your job or catching up on social media, there is so much going on in our lives that takes precedence over a good night's sleep. Sleep is an integral part of a healthy lifestyle. The quality of your sleep directly affects your mental and physical health. It also affects the quality of your life, including your productivity, emotional balance, creativity, and weight. No other activity delivers so many benefits with so little effort.

3. Get Moving

Regular exercise has a profoundly positive impact on your physical and mental health. It trims your waistline, and it can curb depression, relieve anxiety, improve memory, and improve sleep, all of which can boost your overall mood.

You don't have to be a fitness fanatic to reap these benefits. Research indicates that even thirty minutes of exercise per day can make a difference. Joining a group fitness class, working out with a friend, or scheduling a regular workout time are just a few tactics you can use to keep you motivated and inspired to exercise.

4. Find Meaning in Your Work

The career you choose can form part of your identity and shape how you feel about yourself. Working in a job you view as meaningless and directionless can be physically and emotionally draining, regardless of the size of your paycheck or title. While it may not be possible to change your career path, that doesn't mean that you can't still find meaning in your life by restructuring your workday or participating in other gratifying activities like charity work or hobbies. Engaging in gratifications and other flow-producing activities can infuse more meaning into your work, making it more enjoyable.

5. Plug Your Energy Drains

Most of us have a few things in our lives that drain us of our energy every day. These are known as tolerations, and they come in many shapes and forms. They can take the form of a disrespectful coworker or an unresolved conflict with a family member. They can even be small, seemingly inconsequential things like a cluttered table in your home or a clothing alteration you've been putting off. No matter how big or small they may seem, tolerations have a way of accumulating and weighing you down. Learning how to identify and eliminate your tolerations will give you more energy for doing the things you enjoy. Make a list of stressors and then plan to stop them.

6. Make Time for Leisure

Do you ever feel like there is never enough time in the day to do the things you want to do? Yes, life is busy, and most of us have enough work to occupy all of our time—times two—but if you're not allowing yourself time to relax and have some fun, you could be doing yourself a big disservice. Leisure time is more important than many people realize. Research shows that engaging in a leisure activity lowers stress levels, improves mood, and enhances problem-solving skills. Indulge in a pleasurable activity and watch your mood and productivity improve. You might find yourself more energized and excited about doing the things you have to do—or at least not dreading them.

Most of this might seem very generic, right? A generic as it may seem, it is a highly effective plan. Eliminating stressors can be huge. Let us resolve to reconcile the uproar in America over political and ideological differences. If we can spend time understanding these ideologies, we can improve our quality of living. We want to reach a level of peace in understanding to dissolve the thorn of the threat we sometimes feel from the advancement of freedom of speech of others who have opposing views. Let's relax.

Let's not get offended about anything. Let people speak without reaction. A higher quality of life comes from being able to control your emotional side to everything that opposes your own views. This is not easy, and it holds the key to our own personal higher quality of life.

Can we go deeper than that? We know about this emotional trigger from the early part of this book, and political viewpoints can be part of our stressors in life. Let us consider another option for a higher quality of life. How about serving others? How about serving others with different viewpoints? In the end, we just want to be understood and respected.

We may also desire for others to know that we are good people. Most Americans, on either side of the fence, want to be known as good people first and foremost, and their political views do not define their character.

What happens when we begin to serve others? My wife and I volunteered at grieving homes together, and we learned some great things. We learned that death affects everyone in some way, and when death gives its sting, no one cares any longer about the ideologies of life. They seek comfort from anyone. Love finally has its moment without prejudices.

Tears seem to remove roadblocks of empathy or sympathy. Americans historically are great "tear dryers." My wife and I volunteer at a drug addiction home. There are two hundred men at this facility, and our church serves about 50 of them lunch once a month on their graduation out of the program. Guess what? The sting of drug addiction removes ideologies as well. When we serve these men, they appreciate our declaration of love toward them.

Something else begins to happen in this process of serving others. My wife and I began to understand what's important and what is not important. We began to have moments of extreme gratification about how fortunate we are. We also sleep better and relax more in the weeks leading up to these volunteer assignments due to the psyche behind being able to encourage others through their dark times.

We also participate in a prayer tent community outreach. During the prayer tent outreach, we encounter many faith-driven individuals who are seeking to pray for the troubles in their lives. We set up the canopy and table in a CVS parking lot, and many people stop by to share their challenges in life, and we pray for their specific situations. In all the different outreaches we are involved in, it does not matter what anyone's political views are. Pain is open to comfort from anyone.

Each situation has encouraged us more than the people we are able to inspire. I have spent some time doing mission work in Guyana and keep in close communication with many people I have been able to help there. The point of outreach is service to others.

In America, our higher quality of life has always been based on service to others. We fought in wars to help other countries' quality of life. We abolished slavery to try to remove the detestable birthmark of America. We give to third world countries to support the quality of life in those regions. We are a farmland of spiritual fruit to help others enjoy a higher quality of life.

America is great due to all those who came here for a higher quality of life. We, as America, are the very definition of a higher quality of life. How do we accomplish serving others to gain a higher quality of life? I went to Guyana to serve others and came back forever changed as a person. I grew with a great understanding of contentment and appreciation for the luxuries we have access to in America.

Find something positive to be a part of—no matter who you are. Go and see what it looks like in a third world country and learn about the challenges they have—and the joy they still have. Third world countries do not always seem unhappy. Many of the people in these countries are happier than Americans because they are content. We can learn to be thankful and content in our country.

Find a program to join and work on relationships within that organization. Find a passion for something you can help with to positively affect your community. When we feel like contributors, we grow healthier mentally. We must make spiritually development a priority. You can do it. Get started.

God created the human race from one man:

The God who made the world and everything in it is the Lord of heaven and earth and does not live in temples built by human hands. And he is not served by human hands, as if he needed anything. Rather, he himself gives everyone life and breath and everything else. From one man he made all the nations, that they should inhabit the whole earth; and he marked out their appointed times in history and the boundaries of their lands. God did this so that they would seek him and perhaps reach out for him and find him, though he is not far from any one of us. "For in him we live and move and have our being." As some of your own poets have said, "We are his offspring." Therefore since we are God's offspring, we should not think that the divine being is like gold or silver or stone—an image made by human design and skill. In the past God overlooked such ignorance, but now he commands all people everywhere to repent. For he has set a day when he will judge the world with justice by the man he has appointed. He has given proof of this to everyone by raising him from the dead. (Acts 17:24–31 NIV)

ELEVEN

AN ATTITUDE OF GRATITUDE

If we make the choices spoke of in the previous chapter, we should begin to have opportunities of contentment and gratitude. One of the benefits again will be an *Attitude of Gratitude* which improves one's mental health and allows the mind to heal. It will allow our hearts to heal and possibly care more for our neighbors. We might even find ourselves appreciating the relationships of those that are not like us politically, culturally, and of a different race. Gratitude is a huge spiritual posture and it becomes a defining moment of personal growth. Even to an attitude of gratitude towards this great country we live in. I do not have to like Donald Trump to appreciate what efforts he has done for the Economy. I sincerely appreciate his accomplishments. I do not have to like Joe Biden to appreciate that he may have the ability to nurture and Heal America. I do not have to like Mike Pence to be grateful for his service as Vice President of this great nation and to help rationalize some of the efforts and decision that was made by the Trump administration. I do not have to like Kamala Harris to be thankful for her courage to show women of this great nation that they can serve on the largest stage and be inspired for the rest of their lives, that women in leadership are valued in this great country. Gratitude eliminates the threat of perceptions. Gratitude removes the pessimism that reduces the quality of life.

In 1998, I had a very close cousin, who was like a brother to me, that was in a terrible car accident. Due to him being under the influence, he blacked out behind the wheel of his car while going over an overpass and ran into a galvanized light pole. He was pronounced dead on arrival (DOA) at the hospital. He later recovered consciousness at the hospital.

Once my cousin was stabilized, he had eighteen surgeries over six weeks to repair so many areas of his body. After many months of recovery, he finally reached a point where the hospital believed he was at the most stable energy and that they had done the best they could do. When he finally made it home, his mom had to purchase a hospital bed that could help raise him up and down so that she could feed him and change him as needed.

It took several months before he began to speak again. Almost a year later, during one of my many visits with my cousin at his home, we stared at each other, and I wondered if he remembered me. He still was not talking. I suddenly had a great idea, and I went to Circuit City. He had always loved music. I bought a sixty-nine-dollar CD player and three CDs. When I pulled out the CD player, he did not react.

His mom came into the room and said, "Do you think he will enjoy listening to music again?"

I said, "Well, it is worth a try." I put in a CD by a local artist named Fat Pat and begin to play "Tops Drop." My cousin began to shrug his shoulders like if he was dancing in his hospital bed.

His mom started to cry in happiness at this response to the music. He had the biggest smile on his face. After I left that day, his mom would call me and let me know how much she appreciated that radio because his motor skills were getting better each day, and he was pointing at the radio for her to turn it. She said, "Another song, 'A Bunch of Lighters on My Dresser,' moved him and made him smile."

I said, "Aunt, I believe the name of the song is Twenty-Five Lighters on My Dresser." I felt good about that moment with my cousin. We were four years apart, but we had grown up close to each other because our moms were sisters, and we lived in the same neighborhood. I was heartbroken when he had his crash and I cried the moment I was informed. The place where my cousin had the wreck now has a White cross at the spot of the wreck. The city is not aware that he actually survived—or they just decided to leave the White cross there to deter others from driving while intoxicated or under the influence.

By 2001, my cousin had fully recovered from most of his injuries, but he struggled with much of his short-term memory from the crash. He would often sit down with us to say grace before eating at a restaurant, and sometimes he would say grace several times. Once, I said, "You have already said your grace twice—and you can start eating now!"

My cousin looked at me with a smile and said, "It never hurts to say grace again."

I was not spiritually mature and had yet to start going to church regularly.

I agreed with my cousin and thought, *He is right. What is wrong with saying grace several times?*

One Sunday morning my cousin and I were sitting in church together and we had reached the moment in the service where we were supposed to give. As the basket was coming around to our row, I pulled out my wallet and was preparing to give. My cousin pulled out his wallet and was preparing to give as well. I was working for the Union Pacific Railroad, I was making around fifty-two thousand a year plus overtime. I owned a home in Sugarland, which was listed as one of the top ten places to live in America, based on average household income and education level.

My cousin had been permanently disabled since his car wreck and received $515 per month in disability from the government. Before his wreck, he had a girlfriend who was pregnant. It was a blessing that he had a son, and the mother named the son after him. The family greatly appreciated this because we didn't know if my cousin would survive. My cousin was assigned child support—even though he only received $515 per month. His child support was $75 a month, and he only brought home $385 a month after taxes and child support.

As we both were opening our wallets to give in church, I saw a few one-dollar bills, a five-dollar bill, a ten-dollar bill, and a twenty-dollar bill. I wondered which bill I was going to put in the basket as it was getting closer to me. I finally made my selection and picked the five-dollar bill and placed it in the basket. I looked over at my cousin and saw him looking in his wallet with what seemed to be the amount of money. My cousin pulled a twenty-dollar bill out of a side pocket in his wallet and said, "I always put what's God's to the side. When I get my check each month, I cash it and I put four twenty-dollar bills to the side."

I said to him, "In most religions, you only have to give 10 percent."

He said, "Yes, but I am not supposed to be here."

For the rest of the service, I felt somewhat ashamed at my own giving. I thought, *My cousin has a heart of gratitude. He knows that he's lucky to be alive. He also has a son who he can send at least seventy-five dollars per month. He appreciates that he can give God a hundred dollars a month or eighty dollars a month. I have an annual income of fifty thousand, and I am struggling to give God a fraction of what he has given me.*

From that day forward, I begin to give at least twenty dollars every Sunday, which was not even close to 10 percent. I also started saying grace a few times before eating. *It cannot hurt to say it again,* I thought.

People who live with a heart of gratitude appreciate all the little things in life. They live life with more richness each day. If we hang around grateful people, it will either annoy us or become contagious. Let it be contagious and rub off on us. If we desire a higher quality of life, we must adopt a grateful attitude.

What if America has racism in it? Are there no more areas of America to be grateful for? I believe we always have an option or an opportunity to be grateful. We should start each day thankful for all our blessings. This doesn't mean things are perfect or without blemish, but I have a choice in my attitude for the day. Slavery and police brutality should not be allowed to erase America's greatness, and it should not make us ashamed of our country. My cousin was not ashamed of his scars, and he embraced them because they brought him closer to God and yielded joy in his life from a grateful heart.

These few experiences forever changed me with my cousin, and he lives a life much more joyful than I do because he has been blessed to be still alive. He has a wonderful son, who resembles him greatly in personality and features. What's wrong with saying your grace several times. It can't hurt.

My cousin's life was not perfect. America is not perfect, but through our darkness, we gain our most precious character. Before my cousin's car wreck, he had no relationship with God. He had no gratitude, and he lived a fast life and was headed in the wrong direction. He is grateful that he has "a thorn in his side," as stated by the Apostle Paul, and he has embraced it. 2 Corinthians 12:7-10 (NIV) [7] or because of these surpassingly great revelations. Therefore, in order to keep me from becoming conceited, I was given a thorn in my flesh, a messenger of Satan, to torment me. [8] Three times I pleaded with the Lord to take it away from me. [9] But he said to me, "My grace is sufficient for you, for my power is made perfect in weakness." Therefore I will boast all the more gladly about my weaknesses, so that Christ's power may rest on me. [10] That is why, for Christ's sake, I delight in weaknesses, in insults, in hardships, in persecutions, in difficulties. For when I am weak, then I am strong. The thorn in our side becomes like a governor on a four wheeler that keeps you from going to fast. It protects you from harming yourself. Arrogance if not controlled needs a thorn. My CPAP was my thorn in my side. My Sleep Apnea was my thorn. They brought me home each night and stopped me from drinking and or from taking sleeping pills. He is grateful.

America has had some dark days, but it's through darkness that light will appear. What was meant for evil, as Joseph said, but God meant for good. I am grateful to be an American. I understand America went through some dark times to become the land of opportunity today, and I have the option to take advantage of that if I am willing to.

The person who forgets the attitude of gratitude will never be on speaking terms with happiness. An attitude of gratitude is one of the most contagious behavior patterns. Thank you is a therapy that makes people smile and can change an environment. We receive significantly more than we give. It is only with gratitude that life becomes rich. It is easy to overestimate the importance of our own achievements in comparison to what we owe others. There is nothing more hurtful or oppressive than an attitude of ingratitude. What a blow to the spirit! Ungrateful people repel others. A proud attitude does not allow people to feel gratitude. The process of healing in America will depend on how much gratitude we employ in our daily lives. Satan does not want us to become a grateful country because it dissolves his opportunities to divide us as a country. Gratitude does not allow him into the fold. Be grateful—and you will be strong.

While visiting Boston, I saw courage, determination, and sacrifice. It is sometimes called the "Cradle of Liberty" for its role in instigating the American Revolution. Boston's rich history began in the 1630s when the Puritans established a settlement there. Massachusetts's first deputy governor, Thomas Dudley, was from Boston, Lincolnshire, England. Once the capital of the Massachusetts Bay Company, Boston became home to a thousand Puritans who had fled religious and political persecution in Europe. Its inhabitants came to be called Bostonians.

In September 1630, the Puritans landed on the Shawmut Peninsula, so named by the Native Americans who were living there. The Puritans called it Tramontane until the town was renamed after Boston, Lincolnshire, England. The Massachusetts Bay Company's original governor, John Winthrop, preached the famous sermon called "A City Upon a Hill." Before their departure from England in 1630, Winthrop spoke of the special covenant the Puritans had with God and of their actions, which would be watched by the world.

Boston became a hot spot of unrest as the colonists began to rebel against the heavy taxation levied upon them by the British Parliament. The colonists organized a boycott in response to the Townshend Acts of 1767, which resulted in the Boston Massacre. At the trial, it was determined that the redcoats had been drawn to fire upon the crowd. Originally thought to have been the catalyst for swaying the American public against the British, historians recently decided that further unpopular British actions would have had to occur before a larger portion of the populace came to embrace the radical view of independence.

Other upheavals strongly influenced the colonists to raise arms to fight a war against the British. Consider this brief history lesson and see if you agree with the courage, determination, and sacrifice of the Bostonians. Several early Revolutionary War battles were fought in or near Boston. They included the Battles of Lexington and Concord, the Battle of Bunker Hill, and the Siege of Boston. During this period, Paul Revere made his midnight ride.

After the American Revolution, the town became one of the world's wealthiest international trading ports, and descendants from old Boston families became the social and cultural elite called the "Boston Brahmins." In the 1820s, a rush of immigrants from Ireland and Italy began to dramatically change the city's ethnic composition. They brought a staunch Roman Catholicism with them. Catholics currently comprise Boston's largest religious community. The Irish Catholics, in particular have played a significant role in Boston politics, including such prominent figures as John F. Kennedy. If none of these events had taken place, where would America as we know it be today. Better? Does it exist? Can we agree on the events that birthed this nation and the opportunities we have today?

Let's take it a step back further even before Boston. The *Mayflower* carried the Pilgrims from England to Plymouth, Massachusetts, and they established the first permanent New England colony in 1620. Although no detailed description of the original vessel exists, marine archaeologists estimate that the square-rigged sailing ship weighed about 180 tons and measured ninety feet long.

Some sources suggest that the *Mayflower* was constructed in Harwich, England, shortly before English merchant Christopher Jones purchased the vessel in 1608. Some of the Pilgrims were brought from Holland on the *Speedwell*, a smaller ship that accompanied the *Mayflower* on its initial departure from Southampton, England, on August 15, 1620.

When the *Speedwell* proved unseaworthy and was twice forced to return to port, the *Mayflower* set out alone from Plymouth, England, on September 16, after taking on some of the smaller ship's passengers and supplies. Among the *Mayflower's* distinguished voyagers were William Bradford and Captain Myles Standish. Chartered by a group of English merchants called the London Adventurers, the *Mayflower* was prevented by rough seas and storms from reaching the territory that had been granted in Virginia (a region then conceived of as much larger than the present-day state of Virginia, at the time, including the *Mayflower's* original destination in the area of the Hudson River in what is now New York).

After a sixty-six-day voyage, it landed on November 21 on Cape Cod at what is now Provincetown, Massachusetts. On the day after Christmas, it deposited its 102 settlers nearby at the site of Plymouth. Before going ashore at Plymouth, Pilgrim leaders, including Bradford and William Brewster, drafted the Mayflower Compact, a brief two hundred-word document that was the first framework of government written and enacted in the territory that would later become the United States of America. The ship remained in port until the following April when it left for England. The true fate of the vessel remains unknown, but some historians argue that the *Mayflower* was scrapped for its timber, which was then used in the construction of a barn in Jordans, Buckinghamshire, England. In 1957, the historic voyage of the *Mayflower* was commemorated when a replica of the original ship was built in England and sailed to Massachusetts in fifty-three days.

Does this history help at all with gratitude? Does history have any intercession within our hearts to bring an appreciation for the events that let us have the America we know today? If this history lesson failed, let's try another approach. Let's consider the often-forgotten servers of our daily routing in gaining some gratitude.

During the Vietnam War, as F-4 Phantoms hurtled through the air off the aircraft carrier *Kitty Hawk*, a US Navy captain was on his seventy-fifth mission over North Vietnam. From the corner of his eye, he saw the White plume of a surface-to-air missile arching up toward the aircraft. Seconds later, an explosion rocked the aircraft and inverted it.

The captain fought to right the aircraft in order to be able to initiate the ejection system. As the aircraft plummeted to the earth, he somehow got it right side up. He reached over his head with both hands and pulled the ejection shield over his face. The cockpit cover was blown from the aircraft, and a split second later, the rocket under his seat launched him out of the aircraft with a force eighteen times the force of gravity, which was enough to tear off arms and legs that weren't held tight against the body.

After what seemed like an eternity, but was only a few seconds, the seat separated. He heard the parachute canopy inflate with air. He looked up and saw two panels of the parachute had been blown out. Antiaircraft rounds were exploding around him, and the captain started to destroy his flight schedules book, which was procedure, and he searched the ground for a suitable landing place. There was none.

He landed in a rice paddy, and he was surrounded by a group of local farmers who hit him with their shovels and hoes and put him a pen with water buffalo and tried to goad the buffalo to gore him. Fortunately, water buffalos are mostly passive creatures. Then the soldiers arrived—he had landed less than fifty miles from Hanoi—and he began six horrific years as a prisoner of war in North Vietnam.

After 2,103 days in captivity, the captain was repatriated to the United States. He didn't know what would be next as he began the medical care and debriefing processes at the Great Lakes Naval Station. As one of the first POWs returning to the Midwest, he was a bit of a celebrity. Many reporters wanted to learn about his imprisonment and how he was able to cope and survive. Repeatedly, he relived his experience and recounted how his faith in God, self-discipline, and love for America sustained him.

One day, after being interviewed, the captain got on the elevator to go back to his room. Before the door could fully close, a man wedged his shoulder into the door to keep it from closing. He was one of the reporters, and he was crying. He told the captain how much he was feeling sorry for himself until he heard the captain's story. He thanked the captain profusely for sharing and said it had raised him out of his self-pity and changed his life.

The captain thought that maybe there was some value in continuing to share his story. He wanted to positively affect the lives of others as well. Thousands of speeches and presentations later, this US Navy captain continues to inspire and motivate audiences all over the world. This story doesn't end here though. Our subject in this chapter is that of gratitude and remembering the little guy.

The captain and his wife were having dinner in a Kansas City restaurant, and he noticed a man looking at him intently. The man came over to captain's table and asked his name. The captain gave his name, trying to think of who this man was and how he knew of him.

The man said, "You flew jet fighters in Vietnam from the aircraft carrier *Kitty Hawk*. You were shot down! You spent six years as a POW in Vietnam."

"How in the world did you know that?" asked the captain.

"I packed your parachute!"

The captain gasped for air—in surprise and gratitude.

The man vigorously shook his hand and said, "I guess it worked!"

The captain said, "It sure did! If your chute hadn't worked, I wouldn't be here today!"

They reminisced about their service so many years ago.

The captain went back to his room and couldn't sleep that night. He kept wondering what the man had looked like in a navy uniform: a White hat, a bib in the back, and bell-bottom trousers. *I wonder how many times I might have seen him and not even said, "Good morning. How are you?" or anything else because I was a fighter pilot—and he was just a sailor.*

The captain thought of the many hours the sailor had spent at a long wooden table in the bowels of the ship, carefully weaving the shrouds and folding the silks of each chute, holding in his hands each time the fate of someone he didn't know, with the understanding that most likely, the parachute would never be used. However, there was always a chance. Now, when the captain gives his talks, he asks his audience the same powerful question each time he speaks: "Who packed your parachute?" If we are to live in gratitude and joy, we must not forget the little people who pack our parachutes.

Everyone has someone who provides what they need to make it through the day. The captain said he needed many kinds of parachutes that terrible day when his plane was shot down over enemy territory: his physical parachute, his mental parachute, his emotional parachute, and his spiritual parachute. He called on all these chutes before reaching safety. Sometimes in the daily challenges that life gives us, we miss what is really important. We may fail to say hello, please, or thank you. We may forget to congratulate someone on something wonderful that has happened to them, give a compliment, or do something nice for no reason. As you go through this week, this month, or this year, take time to remember and recognize the people who pack your parachutes.

The person who forgets an attitude of gratitude will never be on speaking terms with happiness. Do you agree with this statement? Gratitude depends on joy and is a key component for living a higher quality of life. It is a benefit and not simply a cure for unhappiness. Gratefulness yields joy, which is the title of the next chapter.

In the next chapter, I will reveal how to achieve gratitude. Some people can be given an entire field of roses and only see the thorns, and others can be given a single weed and love the wildflower above it. Positive perception is one of the keys to healing—along with gratitude. Gratitude is conditional for joy to have its day with us. It is not happy people who are thankful. It is thankful people who are happy. What does God have to say? "Over-flow with Thankfulness" Colossians 2:1-10 (NIV) 2 I want you to know how hard I am contending for you and for those at Laodicea, and for all who have not met me personally. ² My goal is that they may be encouraged in heart and united in love, so that they may have the full riches of complete understanding, in order that they may know the mystery of God, namely, Christ, ³ in whom are hidden all the treasures of wisdom and knowledge. ⁴ I tell you this so that no one may deceive you by fine-sounding arguments ⁵ For though I am absent from you in body, I am present with you in spirit and delight to see how disciplined you are and how firm your faith in Christ is.

Spiritual Fullness in Christ

⁶ So then, just as you received Christ Jesus as Lord, continue to live your lives in him, ⁷ rooted and built up in him, strengthened in the faith as you were taught, and overflowing with thankfulness. ⁸ See to it that no one takes you captive through hollow and deceptive philosophy, which depends on human tradition and the elemental spiritual forces of this world rather than on Christ. ⁹ For in Christ all the fullness of the Deity lives in bodily form, ¹⁰ and in Christ you have been brought to fullness. He is the head over every power and authority.

TWELVE

THE JOY OF
AMERICAN CULTURE

In July of 1999 I moved into my first home, that I had put earnest money down on in 1998. It took a year for the completion of the home. My home purchase was in Sugarland Texas, a suburb in southwest Houston. When I was in Junior High School, I had a Reading Teacher that made us write a letter to ourselves with a template that answered a few questions. What College we wanted to attend, what major, what career, where we wanted to live, and if we wanted a family. My letter to myself in 8th grade was that I wanted to attend Texas A&M. I wanted to Major in Accounting and work for Shell Oil as an accountant. This is the career my mother had, and we lived a good life on that salary in the 80's and 90's. Also I stated that I wanted to graduate from college and move to Sugarland Texas.

I grew up in Missouri City Texas which was a neighboring city. After graduation I focused on purchasing my home at 25 years of age, in Sugarland Texas. With the career at Union Pacific during that time I was able to qualify for a home. In 1999-2004 Sugarland Texas was highly rated area to live and, in many years, they were listed at the #4 American City to live in. I often thought to myself that I have accomplished the American dream in a big way. Not that I just purchased a home, but I was able to purchase a home in a city labeled as one of the top 10 places to live in the United States. I purchased a 2 story Pulte home. In the coming years, one of my very close friends asked me if I wouldn't mind using my home for his engagement party, because he had decided against a bachelor party before marriage. I was very proud of him and I told him I was honored to use my home to celebrate his milestone into marriage. I had often thought I would not have a bachelor party as well and when I got married, I did not have a bachelor party. My friend Ron was excited about getting married and he said he just wanted to invite his fraternity brothers, family members, and closest friends to the party. We didn't invite women or any past girlfriends. It was just the closest friends and his fraternity mainly. On that day I decided I would Bar B Que. Being from Texas you would think I was fair at minimum in being able to Bar B Que. This was going to be my first attempt and I was not proficient or knowledgeable at all. I bought all the necessary items to Bar B Que and begin the process in my new back yard of my new home. I was excited and felt good about having a place to hold this engagement party for a childhood friend. Ron and I had been friends since we were 9 years old. We played against each other in little league baseball, ran track together, and played basketball against each other in Junior High. Ron even hit the game winning shot against my junior high team with 10 secs left on the clock. At the end of the game our fathers made us all take pictures together. I started the fire in the Bar B Que Pit and went back into the house to season the meat and get everything prepped. In about 30 Minutes I heard a drastic knock at the door, and it was my neighbor telling me that my back yard was on fire. We both ran to the back yard and grabbed the water hose and started spraying the yard down with water. My neighbor started grabbing buckets of water from inside the house and running to the back yard and pouring it on the flames. Suddenly I became the flame starter, lol. Something I speak against. We were both trying to keep the fire from getting to the fence. We thought if it got to the fence then we would be in trouble of catching other yards on fire and or homes. We finally extinguished the full fire at about a foot from the fence. At this point I didn't think it was a good idea to still attempt to Bar B Que. My first attempt is now an ultimate fail and I still had guest coming over for the Engagement Party. I went into plan B. I started cooking some of the meat in the oven and then ordered Pizza and Wings. Typical male Super Bowl cuisine now. I was able to get some donations from other friends on the additional cost, by providing the humor of my back yard being totally burned down at this point. What a loser I thought, Lol. The engagement party still turned out very well and since 95% of the party was all males, it was just fine.

Around 1:00am as the party was starting to unwind and many of the guest were leaving, some of Ron's fraternity brothers decided to go outside and do what they call some fraternizing. There was a contest they were accustomed to doing between brothers from the same line that pledged. It was a wrestling match where there was a box drawn in an open space and the objective was to push the other fraternity brother outside the lines without allowing him to fall on the ground. Ron and his fraternity brothers asked to use my VHS Recording Camera to film the wrestling match, so they had proof of the winner. This event was going to be done by single elimination and the last man standing would be crowned champion. I begin to clean up my home and throw trash out while they gathered in my front yard for this event. It was 1:00am in the morning and many of my neighbors were sleep for sure and our neighborhood was not completely built out just yet so some of the lots were still empty. After about 40 minutes of this fraternity event taking place in my front yard, I heard a cop car siren and a commotion. I finished washing dishes and begin to go outside. As I was trying to go outside there was an officer on my porch asking for the VHS Camera that Ron had in his hand. Ron backed into the house and the officer did not come in my home. I went outside to speak with the officers and what I saw was chaos. Two of the fraternity brothers were in handcuffs and one of my neighbors was in handcuffs and scratched up. I noticed his watch was shattered on the concrete sidewalk. The officers asked me if I was the owner of the home and I said yes. They let me know they were arresting my friends and that I could go bail them out of jail in Fort Bend County after 3-4 hours. When asked what the charge was, I was told public intoxication and disorderly conduct. Of course, all the witnesses in the yard was saying they were all just playing and fraternizing with each other and there was no harm going on. The officers shared with me that they were called to the seen because it was said someone was fighting. I explained to the officers that I had a degree in Criminal Justice and respected what they do, but I still asked them if they could please let me friends go, and my neighbor go. They told me no because they had already put handcuffs on them and had to book them. I asked the officers politely what my neighbor did, and they said that he was asked to go back home, and he did not. They asked me again for the VHS Camera that was used to film the event and I said I didn't know what had been done with it. After the officers drove off, Ron, others, and I begin making phone calls to the other friends that had been arrested friends and family to help with bailing them all out of jail. I went to my neighbor's house and told his parents what happened and explained how to get him out of jail. These unfortunate situations are not the destroyer of joy in America, but yet they reveal where each side is in their growth as a citizen; even for the police officer involved. Consider these 7 bullets when trying to understand how we should feel and respond. This includes the public and law enforcement.

> ➢ Facts only.
> ➢ Be emotionally intelligent about that communication.
> ➢ Desire no elevated vindication, but change.
> ➢ Evaluate the perceptions of the situation.
> ➢ Understand the cultures involved.
> ➢ Choose not to be offended.
> ➢ Give in to no media propaganda in how you feel.

If we can practice those bullets in our approach, we can possibly have successful and healthy outcomes from some of the most contentious situations today with community and law enforcement. In addition to those bullets above here are few disciplines to go along with that. We should each commit to these set of catalyst for healing in America.

- I am going to listen
- I am going to be kind
- I am going to understand presence of perceptions
- I am going to understand the diversity of cultures exist
- I am "not" going to fan the flames unrest with political propaganda
- I am going to learn to love others (neighbors) that are different from me

What is the takeaway from what was shared? If you are on the outside looking in then just have empathy. Absent of death in these situations we can apply these alternatives to better attitudes after the pain of these situations. Those that have died from similar mishandles by law enforcement has to change. We cannot cultures and traditions to sustain immunity against those lives that were taken by negligence with law enforcement's handling of a situation. Have empathy. The take-away is have empathy. I and my friends were built in such a way that we moved on from this negative experience and no one lost their life in the process. Have empathy with others that are not built with the same grit to just let it go and move on. When we say, "back the blue", understand that backing the blue does not mean we compromise the health and rights of the public. Healing America is about understanding. It was difficult for me to understand why this all happened this way. In the end, things just happen. We must get back up and move on. We cannot live in such a way that we are so far disconnected from understanding, that this event is happening multiple times year over year to different individuals of minorities all over America. This doesn't mean we are being targeted, but it simply means we could be more subject to it, due to tolerances we are not always privileged to when it comes to the racial profile perceptions in standard law enforcement call engagement. We can hope for this change, we can try and influence this change, but we may never achieve this change. We cannot change people; we can change laws to help control people or penalize them for certain actions. We must go there if we desire true change. There is only one bird that pecks an eagle, and that is the crow. The eagle does not defend itself immediately, but instead it simply continues to fly higher and higher and eventually the crow doesn't like that altitude and leaves it alone. The crow then returns to its comfortable altitude and lower levels of living. Eagles rise. America is represented by the eagle for a reason.

Any change, even change for the better, will always be joined by discomfort. We live in a time period when even "living the American dream" is a controversial statement that could be perceived as insensitive and/or ideological. Being a patriot is being noted as a racist or even frowned upon. We have to begin to reject these notions and threats toward gratitude for the country we live in. To be a patriot is honorable. To respect our country is honorable. To love our neighbor is a privilege. We should be grateful not that we have to love our country but that we are so blessed that we get to love our country. I had a boss who always talked about "living the dream."

> Me: Good morning, sir. How are you doing today?
> Boss: Just living the dream.

We even bought him a desk runner with the words "living the dream." The truth is that this statement is simply a factual statement, and if you are grateful and optimistic about life, whoever is open to it can seize the moment.

The American dream is a national ethos in which freedom includes the opportunity for prosperity and success, as well as an upward social mobility for the family and children, achieved through hard work in a society with few barriers. According to the definition of the American dream by James Truslow Adams in 1931, "Life should be better and richer and fuller for everyone, with opportunity for each according to ability or achievement" regardless of social class or circumstances of birth. Of course, we understand through the challenges today there may be advantages with each social class, but the point is still that opportunity exists. The American dream is rooted in the Declaration of Independence, which proclaims that "all men are created equal" with the right to "life, liberty, and the pursuit of happiness." Also, the Constitution promotes similar freedom in the Preamble to "secure the Blessings of Liberty to ourselves and our Posterity."

The American dream is more than a house, two children, and a car in the garage. It's also the idea that Americans can strive for a life of proud individualism, recognition, and personal liberty. One should strive for self-improvement. It has been observed by those both inside and outside of the country that Americans have a penchant for self-education and self-improvement. No one is born knowing how to do everything they need to understand to succeed. To achieve the sort of robust and rugged individualism that is central to the American dream, it's essential to be willing to better yourself wherever and whenever you get the opportunity. Whether it's learning a new skill, practicing a second language, or studying strategies for business success, almost any avenue of self-improvement can help you become a healthier, more versatile, or more productive person.

God gave you a fingerprint that no one else has—so you can leave an imprint that no one else can. When an organic fresh yard egg is broken from the outside, life ends. When an organic fresh yard egg is broken from the inside, life begins. We have to be ready to heal in America, and we have to thrive to break from the inside the patterns of divisiveness that the media and other platforms are sowing in our hearts and minds about our own countrymen. The only victory is in love. There is no other victory here—not right and not left—but love. All that is needed for evil to prevail is for good people to do nothing. It is time to heal America.

Joy is defined by the world as "the emotion evoked by well-being, success, or good fortune or by the prospect of possessing what one desires… the expression or exhibition of such emotion…a state of happiness". This definition of joy is always conditional on circumstance. The biblical or spiritual understanding of 'joy' is very different and is not conditional on circumstance, but a decision to be content and trust God. The joy that the world offers is a pale imitation of the true joy only God can give us. The joy that unsaved people experience is a temporary joy that comes and goes depending on the situation that person is in at the time. For example some lose or gain joy depending what political party is in the presidency. Meaning if its Democrat, then liberals have joy. If its Republican then conservatives have joy. Should this be the driver behind our joy in America?

Why have we given who is in office so much power of our joy? If things are going our way, there is joy. When things are difficult, there is no joy. Consider the poster child for faith in the bible Job. Job's friends utters some insightful words: "…the exulting of the wicked is short, and the joy of the godless but for a moment?" (Job 20:5 ESV cf. 20:18). There can be no true joy apart from God, because Joy Is A Gift From God. Imagine that. Joy comes only from God. Joy is one of the fruits of the Holy Spirit, who resides in the heart of the believer, "But the fruit of the Spirit is love, joy, peace, patience, kindness, goodness, faithfulness…" (Galatians 5:22 ESV). Since God is the author of all things good, when one becomes a Christian, and is united to God through hearing, believing, confessing, baptism, and then living faithfully unto death in Jesus Christ, then the Holy Spirit imparts these qualities to the believer. Have you been baptized today? I encourage you to do so. For unto salvation is yours once you carry-out this action of faith. Joy is also an integral part of the kingdom of God and will exist wherever believers are present, "For the kingdom of God is not a matter of eating and drinking but of righteousness and peace and joy in the Holy Spirit" (Romans 14:17 ESV). So the Joy of American Culture will only come from a person that has allowed the Holy Spirit into their life. Have you allowed the Holy Spirit into your life? Then why are you still in allegiance with politics? Have you allowed the Holy Spirit into your social media posts? Then why are you still dis-respecting the President? Have you allowed the Holy Spirit into your Home? Then why are you teaching your kids there is a wrong and or right political party? There is only Christ and followers of Christ are called Christians. They are not called conservatives or liberals. Have you allowed the Holy Spirit into your decision making? Then why do you not obey authorities put in place by God? Have you allowed the Holy Spirit into your work-space? Then why are you not kinder to your co-workers? In 2020 Covid-19 shocked the world and almost destroyed the economy in the US and shut down all of our hospitality and entertainment nation-wide amongst other privileges we have. Covid-19 can be seen as a "Thorn-In-The-Side" to protect citizens of the US from destroying each other during the 2020 presidential campaign unrest. Covid-19 may have saved us from doing harm to each other. God knows in advance what is needed. The virus took so many lives, but I believed it also saved many from other harms that could have been done during this campaign season.

We will now have a vaccine for this virus. There will still be another virus in this nation un-cured. The only vaccine for that virus of being mean, unkind, and judgmental towards one another is Christ. Love Thy Neighbor is the cure/vaccine. See we can still find gratitude and joy if we just try and be content with God's plan over our plan. Doing God's Will Increases Our Joy. Services to others increases our joy. We prayed for who we wanted in office and not who God wanted in office. We trusted our understanding over his understanding.

As many Christians can attest, being involved in the spread of the Gospel brings joy to the believer's heart. Why do we share more political views than the Gospel? How do others know we are Christian? They know our political stance. Personally, when I see someone become a <u>follower of Jesus</u> or I know that someone has discovered a truth from God's Word that will encourage him or her in their walk of faith, I cannot help but feel a sense of joy. The apostle Paul also experienced this often in his ministry (II Corinthians 1:24, 2:3; Philippians 1:4, 2:2; I Thessalonians 2:19, 20, 3:9; II Timothy 1:4; Philemon 1:7; and many other passages). The writer of Third John experienced the joy of ministry, "I have no greater joy than to hear that my children are walking in the truth" (3 John 1-4 ESV). Amen Goes There! If we want to experience the "Joy" of American Culture, put down politics and pick up faith and go love someone today. Joy is healing revealed. It is the post effect of a person that has healed. Joy comes after healing has taken its course. Everyone that Jesus healed walked away with Joy. Do you have Joy today? Get out the ring! This is not your fight. Go and be glad in today as Jammer's Peer advised him of in the first chapter of this book.

Circumstances Cannot Take Away Our Joy. In Second Corinthians 6:10, Paul says that Christians can even be "sorrowful, yet always rejoicing" (ESV). This means that even when we are in the midst of a situation that legitimately brings us sorrow, our inner joy is never taken away. The very core of our being can still rejoice in the fact that we are forgiven children of God who enjoy an intimate relationship with the Creator of the universe. Our joy is strengthened when we remember that, no matter what the circumstances, God is with us and He is above all.

The only thing that can steal our joy Is sin. The outcome of an election cannot steal our joy. It is not trusting in God as our caregiver that steals our joy. Godly joy is a wonderful thing; it is a supernatural gift from God to every believer. However, one warning must be issued. <u>Sin</u> can steal our joy. It is difficult to experience the joy of our relationship with God when we have done something that damages that relationship. Joy is a gift of the Holy Spirit; when we grieve the Holy Spirit by our sin, we interfere with the flow of joy (among other things) from God. If we find that we are experiencing joy less and less, we may need to reevaluate our relationship with Jesus Christ to make sure we are living as we should.

Opportunity requires one to work hard. Almost everyone can agree that achieving your dreams in America requires hard work. This is not a place of opportunity and fortune absent of effort. It requires effort, focus, and a plan. All this is a benefit of being an American. Most people will say, "Just give me a shot!" America does just that. It gives a person a shot.

A poll found that almost 90 percent of respondents agreed that a strong work ethic is "absolutely essential" for living the American dream. You may be aiming to climb from humble beginnings like Jammer, want a comfortable, middle-class life, ascend from the middle class to the upper class, or even rise from the very bottom to the highest echelons of society. You will be given that opportunity here.

You need a powerful personal drive to achieve. Getting ahead in life means what it sounds like: working hard so that you can pull ahead of those who put in only an ordinary level of effort. For starters, you may want to try working harder and longer than other people at your job. Simple things help advance a person. Most employees will usually leave as soon as the end of the workday hits. They don't offer to stay late or do something it if it is not appropriate for that career. If others slack during their downtime, consider taking on additional job assignments. Do not be discouraged by those who tease you or call you a brownnoser or a teacher's pet. Working harder than other people around you is an excellent way to get noticed at work, and eventually, you will reap the rewards with promotions and raises. In America, it can happen. In most cases, it *will* happen!

In America, there has been a generational shift, and the generation has learned to work smarter. They have learned to work more efficiently without compromising quality. In America, it's much better to be recognized for being exceptionally efficient and productive than being content to spend lots of effort at tasks that can be accomplished more easily in other ways.

Always be striving to improve your efficiency, especially at work. "How can I do my job quicker?" "How can I do it more simply?" "How can I do it with less effort?" Do not compromise on quality. Opportunity benefits everyone. It is what makes American great.

I am comforted to know that my kids have opportunities. It is up to me as a parent to coach them up in this society to seize the opportunities they have before them. I taught them respect of country, consideration of cultures, respect of people, respect of authority, and respect of self. These are the values that bring achievement and long-term success.

Respect is fruitful. We should all have active civic lives. Get involved in the community and the voting process. Be engaged with democracy. Use your voice to help improve matters of contention. Lead with a "we" state of mind. Lead through service. The United States was established on the foundation of representative democracy. The more people who are involved in the process of voting, the more genuinely representative the nation's government will be of its diverse citizens. All Americans who can vote should make sure they do so. However, this is far from the only way to actively participate in the country's civic life. As we move to a healed state, we should be able to agree with much of what has been said. We cannot convince everyone that America is great, but those who are living with gratitude in their hearts, respect in their minds, and love for others will agree. Where do we go from here? Put things into play. Let us grow. Let us heal. There is no *they*. There is only *we*. America is one team.

We are ready to face the outcome of the 2020 election. Who will it be? I will say it again, can Donald Trump or Joe Biden nurture this nation while also sustaining the current momentum of a thriving economy? Is capitalism greater than nurturing or do they both hold the same importance? If you are reading this today, then this decision has already been made, by God and by the general public and the voting procedures set forward by our democracy. Who will help us heal? When we worry, we suffer twice. No worries here. The only two things we are in control of are our attitudes and our responses to the daily media, social media, and the outcome of the 2020 election.

We live in such a way that we are so afraid of losing certain rights in

America that we eventually lose creditability, which should be the greater of the two fears. The fear of losing the lesser will soon lead to the reality of losing the greater.

"So, whatever you wish that others would do to you, do also to them, for this is the Law and the Prophets." (Matthew 7:12 ESV) How does the Golden Rule of Christianity change everything? If you've been a Christian for very long, chances are you've had to endure a legalistic Bibles Study at least once or twice. They normally start out like this, "Where does the Bible say it's wrong to _____?" And with that the battle begins. Obscure, proof texts are interjected (and usually pulled out of context, I might add) to either prove or disprove a position. If we could only hear the voice of our Savior Jesus Christ in this text, things would be greatly simplified, and this madness would quickly end. It's not complicated. Jesus lays down a clear principle (we call it "The Golden Rule") that effectively cuts through all the legalistic hairsplitting, taking us to the very heart of the Law. The Golden Rule is undergirded by the two great commandments (Matthew 22:34-40). If we love God sincerely with all our heart and genuinely love our neighbor as ourselves, then there has been a fundamental change in our thought process. We no longer think about our *"rights"* or what is merely "allowable" anymore. All such selfish thoughts have been put to death. All that concerns us now is what is best for others, and what, ultimately, will bring the most glory to God. The Golden Rule, therefore, is a paradigm shift in the way we think about things. When this shift takes place, we think only in terms of what is best for God and others instead of what we feel the Law might allow. Right wing Christians find themselves in the core of arguments that are all worldly and not of the spirit declaring what they are personally entitled to and afraid of losing and during these times they have nailed Jesus back to the cross in the process. Love, love the Master is saying. Love others. Love Neighbor. Liberal is not absent of deleted from this approach in love as well. It is available to all. Christians on both sides of the fence, arguing and demonizing each other for sake of party. No, No, No. All the Law and the Prophets hang on these two commandments. A new commandment I give you: Love one another, as I have loved you, so also you must love one another. (John 13:34 NIV)

The mission to heal is not entirely on the president and the administration; it is more significantly on each person who decides they want to heal and help others heal. One could argue that the mission to heal is on the Christian. In reality, this will be the process that will work.

Do we continue in vindication or try to understand? Joe Biden and Kamala Harris are confirmed challengers. Trump and Pence are strong and steady on the economy. All candidates are Americans at the end of the day, and they have many common areas of agreement. Perceptions are high. Let us begin to utilize the approaches to healing today. Many people resist change because they are afraid of what they have to give up. Failure to see what you could gain will ultimately lead to our demise. We can, we will, we must….. Heal America.

What does God have to say? Joy

Joy is a state of mind and an orientation of the heart. It is a settled state of contentment, confidence, and hope. It is something or someone that provides a source of happiness. It appears 88 times in the Old Testament in 22 books; 57 times in the New Testament in 18 books.

According to Webster's Dictionary, joy is experiencing great pleasure or delight. Joy is a state of mind and an orientation of the heart. It is a settled state of contentment, confidence, and hope. It is something or someone that provides a source of happiness. It appears eighty eight times in the Old Testament in twenty-two books and fifty-seven times in the New Testament in eighteen books.

Christians should always find reasons to be joyful. There are so many ways to define joy. Joy isn't just a smile or a laugh. Joy is something that is deep within and doesn't leave quickly. When we have the joy of the Lord, we'll know it—and so will others. Since joy is given by God and is something that he wants us to have, we need to be joyful! In addition to being optimistic, we should let others have joy and not bring them down when they are excited about good things. The only thing worse than not having joy is stealing someone else's joy.

Spending eternity in heaven with God, the saints, and the angels will be incredible! Ask for joy! If we can't find reasons to be joyful, our perspectives must change. God lets us have blessings every day. We should be able to see them and thank God for them. Additionally, we should ask for God's blessings! Some people think they should be blessed with joy automatically, but God's Word says, "You have not because you do not ask" (John 15:16).

God's Holy Spirit produces joy. Joy is a product of being Christlike. When we seek God through His Word and our prayers, we will receive joy! Thank God that joy is something he wants us to have!

Joy is the second fruit of the Spirit:

But the fruit of the Spirit is joy. (Galatians 5:22)

Reading the scriptures will bring us joy:

> And these things we write to you that your joy may be full. (1 John 1:4 NIV)

We will also see where the Bible gives us specific times to be joyful. I've listed ways that God has given me joy! If you're lacking, pray and try some of them! Enjoy this lesson—and God bless you!

Peace and joy go together. Give good advice and give friendly advice. When we try not to fight and hate others and decide to get along, we will experience peace and joy:

> Rejoice in the Lord always. I will say it again: Rejoice! (Philippians 4:4 NIV)

> Deceit is in the heart of those who devise evil, but counselors of peace have joy. (Proverbs 12:20 NIV)

> It is a joy for the just to do justice, but destruction will come to the workers of iniquity. (Proverbs 21:15 NIV)

> For God gives wisdom and knowledge and joy to a man who is good in His sight; but to the sinner He gives the work of gathering and collecting, that he may give to him who is good before God. This also is vanity and grasping for the wind. (Ecclesiastes 2:26 NIV)

Rejoice with those who rejoice, and weep with those who weep. (Romans 12:15)

Section 4 - Social Challenge

Take someone to lunch twice that has different views as you. Maybe you two or of various political parties, different religions, or races. Identify a person you know for sure you may not have a lot in common with and invite them out to lunch. Then you must do it a 2nd time. That person has to also invite someone out twice that they have identified. Whoever you invite out for lunch, you pick up the tab both times. Post a picture of the outing on social media and briefing of why you chose them and anything you would like to share about the time spent with them at lunch. Try to learn and have a dialogue about current events and get to know each other. Allow peace and love to have a moment in the encounter. Grow by getting to know someone with alternative thought about America. Ask about career, kids, spouse, family life etc. Make it a small fellowship. Start you a list of 5 individuals you are considering. Pick 1 or more. Share it all. Someone else my grow or be encouraged by your encounter.

CLOSING

Let us move back to the vision in our introduction and recast the events that were taking place. The doctor entered the room with Lady Liberty, and the commoners who have been more ill than she has been in quite some time were asked a powerful question: "Do you want to heal?"

The question is simple but decadent. If the answer is yes, then you have finished reading this book. I want to refer to our scripture in the introduction. As we recall, the man who Jesus asked if he wanted to be healed gave many excuses for why he had not been healed. The reality is that the man had not done anything about it:

> Jesus said to him, "Get up, take up your bed, and walk." And at once the man was healed, and he took up his bed and walked. Now that day was the Sabbath. So the Jews said to the man who had been healed, "It is the Sabbath, and it is not lawful for you to take up your bed." But he answered them, "The man who healed me, that man said to me, 'Take up your bed, and walk.'" They asked him, "Who is the man who said to you, 'Take up your bed and walk'?" Now the man who had been healed did not know who it was, for Jesus had withdrawn, as there was a crowd in the place. Afterward Jesus found him in the temple and said to him, "See, you are well! Sin no more, that nothing worse may happen to you." The man went away and told the Jews that it was Jesus who had healed him. And this was why the Jews were persecuting Jesus because he was doing these things on the Sabbath. But

Jesus answered them, "My Father is working until now, and I am working." (John 5:8–15 NIV)

What would have happened to this man if he had not taken up his bed and walked? What was this man's sin that Jesus spoke of here? Notice how many of the people did not offer up encouragement because they wanted to locate the person they believed had done something wrong on the Sabbath.

It will be the same way today if you decide to change and take up your bed and walk. You will begin to heal, but misery will make you stay in your current state, on the ground, and feel powerless. Jesus gives us the power to go. So, it is time to get up and go. Replace the Elephant and Donkey with the Lamb. Many of the people in the room with Lady Liberty were not so much the enemy, but they could be enemies of each other—based on perceptions or the desire to be vindicated or justified. That doesn't allow progress and growth. They must learn to listen to each other and have kindness in their approaches toward each other. All the examples given to America by the Lamb in the Holy Scriptures. From there, the healing will begin. There are no excuses. The man at the pool had many excuses. America we must move from our current state to a healed state. We must decide to change our ways of thinking and move toward the healing process in love for God, humanity, and country and let all of this be over party. Amen.

REFERENCES

"John 5 ESV—The Healing at the Pool on the Sabbath." https://www.biblegateway.com/passage/?search=john%205&version=ESV.

"Culture vs. History." VS Pages. http://vspages.com/culture-vs-history-2753/.

"With Great Power Comes Great Responsibility—Quote." https://quoteinvestigator.com/2015/07/23/great-power/.

"Captain America: Civil War | Superheroes at odds." http://jamaica-gleaner.com/article/entertainment/20160504/captain-america-civil-war-super-heroes-odds.

"Captain America: Civil War (2016)—Plot Summary." IMDb. https://www.imdb.com/title/tt3498820/plotsummary.

"What Does 'Evangelical' Really Mean? 10 Things to Know." https://www.christianity.com/church/denominations/what-does-the-term-evangelical-really-mean-here-are-10-things-to-know.html.

"What Do the Russians Have on the Trump Family?" https://www.esquire.com/news-politics/politics/news/a56218/trump-junior-russian-meeting/.

"Frequently Requested Statistics on Immigrants and …" https://www.migrationpolicy.org/article/frequently-requested-statistics-immigrants-and-immigration-united-states-7.

"Luke 12:48." Bible Gateway. https://www.biblegateway.com/verse/en/luke+12:48.

"How did God respond when Solomon asked for wisdom." https://www.gotquestions.org/Solomon-wisdom.html.

"1 Timothy 2:1–7 Fear God. Honor the Emperor (McLarty …" https://sermonwriter.com/sermons/1-timothy-21-7-fear-god-honor-emperor-mclarty/.

Wikipedia s.v. "scapegoat." https://en.wikipedia.org/wiki/Scapegoat.

"War of the Worlds Essay—Perception is defined as the …" https://www. coursehero.com/file/53600357/War-of-the-Worlds-Essay/.

Nez Perce County Democrats, 618C D St., Lewiston, ID (2020). https:// www.govserv.org/US/Lewiston/123241815409/Nez-Perce-County-Democrats.

"Media's Influence on Public Perception of Law Enforcement." https:// www.bartleby.com/essay/Media-s-Influence-On-Public-Perception-Of-FKBD5L5ZLJ5Q.

Korten, David. "Ecological Civilization and the New Enlightenment." *Tikkun* 32, no. 4 (October 2017): 17.

"Understanding and Defining White Privilege." https://www.thoughtco. com/white-privilege-definition-3026087.

Dictionary.com, s.v. "characters." https://www.dictionary.com/browse/ characters.

Dictionary.com, s.v. "content." https://www.dictionary.com/browse/content.

Wikipedia, s.v. "Moral character." https://en.wikipedia.org/wiki/Moral_character.

Vocabulary.com, s.v., "character." https://www.vocabulary.com/dictionary/ Character.

"The Gradual Erosion of Whiteness." *Nashville Post*. https://www.nashvillepost. com/business/blog/20415263/the-gradual-erosion-of-whiteness.

"The End of White America?" American Renaissance. https://www.amren. com/news/2009/01/the_end_of_whit_1/.

"Denver police officer fired for 'Let's start a riot' post." https://www. sfgate.com/news/article/Colorado-governor-mayor-Trump-threat-is-15310710.php.

"160 Years of Atlantic Stories." *The Atlantic*. https://www.theatlantic.com/ projects/160-years/.

"Three of the Best YA Books About Basketball." Book Riot. https:// bookriot.com/2019/10/09/ya-books-about-basketball//

Wikipedia, s.v. "White Americans." https://en.wikipedia.org/wiki/White_Americans.

"Going Where Glenn Beck Wouldn't: Defining White Culture." https:// www.huffpost.com/entry/going-where-glenn-beck-wo_b_663303.

Wikipedia, s.v. "Jane Elliott." https://wiki2.org/en/Jane_Elliott.

"One Nation Divided Over a Movement: Your Life Matters." https://colorfulchaos.blog/?p=4769&cpage=1.

"West Midlands Police Positive Action—Posts" Facebook. https://www.facebook.com/West-Midlands-Police-Positive-Action-111526773714479/posts/.

"Associated Press Because of the Associated Press article ..." https://www.coursehero.com/file/p1h1eio/Associated-Press-Because-of-the-Associated-Press-article-Elliott-was-invited-to/.

"Audio." Rhymes World. http://rhymesworld.com/id8.html.

"A riot is the language of the unheard, Martin Luther." https://theweek.com/speedreads/917022/riot-language-unheard-martin-luther-king-jr-explained-53-years-ago.

"Minneapolis protest: Martin Luther King Jr. quote about ..." https://www.usatoday.com/story/news/nation/2020/05/29/minneapolis-protest-martin-luther-king-quote-riot-george-floyd/5282486002/.

Acceptance Address for the Nobel Peace Prize | The Martin ... https://kinginstitute.stanford.edu/king-papers/documents/acceptance-address-nobel-peace-prize.

"Was Martin Luther King Jr. a Republican or a Democrat?" https://www.britannica.com/story/was-martin-luther-king-jr-a-republican-or-a-democrat.

"AOC and the blind generation." Godlike Productions. https://www.godlikeproductions.com/forum1/message4146840/pg1.

Reynolds, John Mark N. "Vindicate God." https://www.patheos.com/blogs/eidos/2018/02/vindicate-god/.

"Biomedical Engineering Inventions." Rocketswag. http://www.rocketswag.com/anatomy/medicine-branch/biomedical-engineering/Biomedical-Engineering-Inventions.html.

"God & Natural Law." Answers in Genesis. https://answersingenesis.org/is-god-real/god-natural-law/.

"Family." Church of Jesus Christ. https://www.churchofjesuschrist.org/study/manual/for-the-strength-of-youth/family?lang=eng.

"AT&T's CEO gives a forceful defense of Black Lives Matter." https://www.chicagotribune.com/business/ct-att-ceo-black-lives-matter-20160930-story.html.

"Watch AT&T's CEO give a forceful defense of Black Lives Matter."
https://www.washingtonpost.com/news/the-switch/wp/2016/09/30/
watch-atts-ceo-give-a-forceful-defense-of-black-lives-matter/.

"Discover 6 Levels of Emotional Maturity & Responsibility." https://
kevinfitzmaurice.com/free-stuff/responsibility-issues/the-6-levels-
of-emotional-maturity/.

"Three Questions to Ask Yourself." HECM World.com. https://hecmworld.
com/reverse-mortgage-news/reverse-professional-career-purpose/.

"Snowflakes." Trap Shooters Forum. https://www.trapshooters.com/
threads/snowflakes.820567/.

"How to Choose to Not Be Offended." http://www.jeremystatton.com/
offense.

"How to Choose to Not be Offended." Choosing Wisdom. https://www.
choosingwisdom.org/choose-not-offended/.

Wikipedia, s.v. "Quality of life." https://en.wikipedia.org/wiki/Life_
quality.

"How to Improve Your Quality of Life." Verywell Mind. https://www.
verywellmind.com/how-to-maintain-a-high-quality-of-life-3144723.

"Mayflower | History, Voyage, & Facts." Britannica. https://www.
britannica.com/topic/Mayflower-ship.

"Staunton Park Genealogy Heritage Centre." Facebook. https://www.
facebook.com/Staunton-Park-Genealogy-Heritage-Centre-1381243
998573647/posts/.

Trammell McGee-Cooper. "Who Packed Your Parachute." http://amca.
com/amca/wp-content/uploads/Who-Packed-Your-Parachute.pdf.

"How to Live the American Dream (with Pictures)." WikiHow. https://
www.wikihow.com/Live-the-American-Dream.

ABOUT THE AUTHOR

Houston native that holds an assortment of titles. Christian. Husband of Gwendolyn Blount and father of three wonderful kids. Over 21 years Client Solution Executive at AT&T. Cyber Security Certification. Minister Certification. Real Estate Broker. Criminal Justice Degree. Now Author.

Printed in the United States
By Bookmasters